# Gary Player, World Golfer

# Gary Player, World Golfer

*His Autobiography*

with
Floyd Thatcher

PELHAM BOOKS

First published in Great Britain in 1975
by PELHAM BOOKS LTD
52 Bedford Square, London WC1B 3EF

First Published by Word Books, Waco, Texas



ISBN: 0 7207 0871 0

Printed in Great Britain by
Hollen Street Press Ltd at Slough, Bucks
and bound by Dorstel Press at Harlow, Essex

# Contents

# Preface

On my first trip to the United States in 1957 it took me forty-six hours of exhausting flying time from my home in Johannesburg. Today it takes only nineteen hours of comfortable travel. Quite a change!

There have been many changes as the world has become smaller and more complex. Living together in a sort of global neighbourhood isn't particularly easy. Cultural differences, tensions, and misunderstandings, both among individuals and nations, have had us at a standoff so often. But in my more than four million miles of travel across the world during the past twenty years, I've discovered a common trait among people everywhere: the desire for inner and outward peace and fulfilment – love for self and others.

Writing this book has been a new and interesting experience as I've attempted to put into words my deepest thoughts and feelings against the framework of my own background and life. Playing professional golf and striving to be the best in the world has demanded an intensive kind of personal discipline. But I've found that to be truly successful in the world of golf one must first come to accept himself as a human being who has the inner capabilities to improve and become a better person. Somewhere I read this powerful comment, and it expresses my own belief so well: 'What men think is the inner force that shapes what they are and do.'

I think, too, that an authentically successful person – golfer or businessman or housewife – is one who has learned to respect and love other people. True, there is a lot of hate, suspicion, and inequality around, but there's also much that is right with the world today if we look for it. Certainly I can't condone any form of social injustice. People of every race or creed must have equal opportunity, and I will continue to work for them in my own way. But the universal principle remains the same: every one of us needs the acceptance and love of other people – to receive we must give.

At least in my own experience, faith in God has been the central force in everything that happens. In saying all of this, however, I certainly don't set myself up as a paragon of virtue nor do I mean to imply in any way that I've arrived at any lofty place or am a candidate for sainthood. Quite the opposite is true. I make my share of mistakes – more than I like – but I'll never give up and I intend to keep trying.

It's my business to hit a little white ball across wide expanses of green grass on golf courses around the world under all sorts of conditions. Playing golf well is an art . . . a skill . . . a profession, and I'm proud of it. But of even greater importance is what I believe to be my calling as an ambassador of goodwill to people in many countries. Getting to know them, working and playing with them, prompts understanding and love. And in addition to my own loved ones and friends, thousands of these people have helped form the thoughts and phrases of this book.

*Gary Player*

*November 1974*
*Johannesburg, South Africa*

# 1 Visualize winning

*I saw something no one else could see . . .*

Posted on the giant leaderboard at Bellerive Country Club in St. Louis in 1965 were the names of all previous United States Open winners. And emblazoned in bright gold at the top of the list was the 1964 champion, Ken Venturi. But every day as I walked past that large board, I *saw* something no one else could see . . . yet. No mistake about it. Right at the top, just above Venturi's name and in bold headline type, it read: 1965 – Gary Player.

Jack Nicklaus and I had flown to St. Louis a week early for a run of practice rounds on the Bellerive course. And we practised long and hard every day, spending hours on the course and the practice tee. The 7,191-yard Robert Trent Jones course was the longest on which a United States Open Championship had ever been played up to that time. The press somewhat doggedly insisted that it was made to order for powerhouse hitters like Nicklaus and Palmer. I knew, though, it wasn't the length of the course but its toughness that had to be beat. The treacherous six-inch-deep Bermuda roughs, seventy-four strategically placed sand traps, tricky water hazards, and slick, oversized greens would test the nerve and skill of the greatest golfers. Everything indicated that course conditions were almost certain to rule out any possibility of a sub-par tournament.

Reports were rife that not many forecasters gave me much of a chance of winning because I had competed in only seven

*Bellerive Country Club, Saint Louis, Missouri, site of 1965 United States Open, won by Gary Player With this championship, Gary became only the third man ever to win golf's Grand Slam, and sentimental association resulted in his naming his South African ranch Bellerive. View at left with clubhouse in background is of the 17th green.*

other United States tournaments up to that point in 1965. But I was ready – physically and mentally. To win this tournament would fulfil a dream that had haunted me from the moment I turned professional in 1953 right up to this middle week of June 1965. It was the final leg in the Grand Slam of golf for me which began six years earlier when I won the British Open at Muirfield in 1959. Capturing the prestigious American Masters title in 1961 and the dramatic United States PGA in 1962 had taken me three-quarters of the way. But until now the United States Open title had been elusive.

Only two men in the history of golf, durable and indefatigable Gene Sarazen and brilliant and courageous Ben Hogan, had achieved the signal honour of winning the Grand Slam. I was determined to become number three – an ambitious dream for a twenty-nine-year-old miner's son from South Africa. But it *was* my dream, and it persisted with all the tenacity of a terrier pup hanging onto an old sock. Sarazen and Hogan were superstars of golf; they had fought and clawed their way to the pinnacle of success. Nothing less would satisfy me.

On the way to the first tee on opening day I hesitated for a few moments in front of the leaderboard, still visualizing my name in the 1965 winner's spot. Briefly I prayed, 'Dear God, give me strength and courage to try my best and fight it out as hard as I can and to accept things in adversity.' When I took a bogey five on the very first hole, it looked like the adversity part of that prayer just might become reality.

But things levelled off, and after the first two days of play the 150-man field narrowed down to 50. The notorious 6th hole, a deceptively simple 195-yard par-3 protected by three sand traps and a pond, had exacted a frightful toll both days. Seventy-seven balls had splashed down into the water, and the record books recorded an unbelievable 211 strokes over par. Arnold Palmer, with a 152, and Ken Venturi, the defending champion, with a humiliating 160, missed the cut and headed for home. Jack Nicklaus had drifted back into the pack and out of contention with a 150. At this point my two rounds totalled

*The green of the notoriously treacherous par-3 6th hole, where the pond caught 77 balls during the first two days of tournament play.*

140, just one stroke ahead of Kel Nagle of Australia and Mason Rudolph.

My belief that distance on this course was not so important had proved correct. If I may say so, we non-American golfers have a bit of an advantage, because we're accustomed to playing on courses where the roughs are much higher and thicker than on American courses. This means that we must first learn to hit the ball straight – then we can concentrate on distance. The Bellerive roughs were formidable. To drift into them was pure trouble.

On Saturday the weather continued clear, warm, and beautiful; the long fairways and silky smooth greens were in perfect condition and the galleries just couldn't have been friendlier. Play slogged along in a fairly routine pattern except for my only birdie of the day on the 14th hole, a dogleg par-4. My tee shot drifted too far left, leaving an exceptionally difficult second shot with a tree between the ball and the flag stick. Using a 7-iron, I started the ball about forty yards to the right and then hooked onto the green, stopping just three feet short of the pin. From there I holed out in 3 and closed the day with a 71, still holding a two-stroke lead over Nagle.

Before starting play on Sunday morning I called my wife, Vivienne, in Johannesburg and learned that our four oldest children were going around with thumbs folded into their fists for good luck. They, of course, are my most enthusiastic fans and really get up tight when I'm playing a big tournament. Then, as I walked past the leaderboard on my way to the 1st tee, I could still *see* my name in the winner's spot. All week long I had been reading and studying *The Power of Positive Thinking* by Norman Vincent Peale, and what he had to say made a lot of sense to me. His words 'visualize winning' were etched deeply in my mind. This had been my pattern for many years, but now the techniques for visualizing a goal emerged in concrete form.

In spite of Sunday's intense heat I played very well. After fifteen holes my lead over Kel Nagle had lengthened to three strokes. I recall walking down the 15th fairway with Mr. Hardin of the United States Golf Association and that he said, 'Well, you've got it all locked up.' And I remember replying, 'No, you can never say that until the last putt has been holed.' I was so right!

On 16 my 4 wood off the tee nosed right into a bunker. Somehow this seemed to trigger disaster, and before finishing the hole I'd taken a double bogey. And to make matters worse, just as I walked off the green, the news squawked through the walkie-talkie that Nagle had birdied 17. My three-stroke lead had dissolved, and now we were even. The heat was on and I knew it.

After parring 17, I moved on toward the tee box at 18, my mind clouded with dark, negative thoughts. 'This is terrible. Am I going to be like Sam Snead?' Sam had won the Masters three times, the PGA Championship three times, and the British Open once. But he had never been able to capture the United States Open Championship, although, interestingly enough, over the years Sam has won 84 PGA titles and a total of 137 around the world.

But as I concentrated, the positive side of my mind began to take over. I had to have a par on 18 to stay even with Kel, but a birdie would give me the one-stroke lead needed to win. Why not try for it?

The 18th at Bellerive is a tough par-4 – trees on the left, out of bounds on the right. My drive landed in excellent position on the right side of the fairway, and a 5-iron second shot came to rest on the green just fifteen feet from the hole. Then came that big moment of truth. After studying the greens, I sighted the putt carefully, and then . . . it moved right along a line directly toward the cup but faltered to a stop just a fraction short. It's true golf is a game of inches, but this was unreal.

At that moment I missed winning the United States Open Championship by one and one-half inches. My easy tap-in insured a tie with Nagle at 282 – two strokes over par – and we were headed for an 18-hole playoff the next day. *Visualize winning?* I still was, but it would have to wait.

I went into Monday's round feeling good and hitting well. After four holes I was leading Nagle by one stroke. The pressure he felt as he teed up for number 5 must have been tremendous, for disaster struck. Kel's drive arced badly and bopped a woman spectator right on the head. Blood poured from her scalp as she toppled over unconscious. I tried to reassure Kel: 'Don't let it get you.' But obviously shaken and unnerved, he moved up to the ball again and this time blasted a grass-cutter that ricocheted off another woman's ankle. The remaining thirteen holes slipped by without much excitement, at least when compared to number 5.

The results after eighteen holes: Player, 71; Nagle, 74. The

United States Open, America's biggest golf championship, was mine . . . all mine. It had not been won by a foreign player since Ted Ray captured the title in 1920 – forty-five years before.

With this win I had joined ranks with Gene Sarazen and Ben Hogan. Now there were three members of the gilt-edged Grand Slam club . . . and I was one of them. This had to be one of the happiest moments of my life.

In 1962, while walking toward the 18th green at Oakmont, I had promised Joe Dye of the United States Golf Association that if I ever won the United States Open, I'd donate my winnings to charity. That was a promise I was glad to make good on this day in 1965. From my United States Open purse of $25,000, $20,000 went to the USGA to help promote junior golf and $5,000 to the Cancer Fund for research in memory of my mother. In addition I paid my caddie $2,000. My words at that moment expressed my deepest feelings, then and now: 'I'm a foreigner here. The American people have treated me so well that I want to give something back.'

# 2 A rich heritage

*It's what's inside that matters.*

Nine years before that dramatic win at Bellerive in St. Louis I had thoughtfully laid out six major goals for myself: having the lowest stroke average for an entire year on the United States professional golf tour, being the top money winner on the U.S. circuit for a year, winning the British Open, the American Masters, the United States PGA Championship, and the United States Open Championship.

True, those were high ambitions for a young South African, twenty years old, but I've always been very serious about both my golf career and my goals in life. Five of those aspirations had come true before St. Louis; winning the United States Open in 1965 was number six. In a way it was a bit frightening for all of that to happen before I was thirty years old. And there were those harbingers of gloom who predicted that I would let down, play less, and eventually devote myself entirely to our family interests in South Africa. But I have always believed deeply that my desire and ability to play golf were God-given. With this in mind I was determined to set new goals and broaden my influence as a golfer and as a person throughout the world.

My flight home from St. Louis to Johannesburg took on a special quality this time. It has become quite a routine thing for me to hop a plane somewhere in the world for the long flight home. And it is still a long flight even though it takes only nineteen hours now as compared to forty-seven for my first flight to the United States. But my stomach is always a little jumpy with the anticipation of seeing my family again. Even now, with millions of miles and years of travel behind me, I find it terribly hard to be away from home and separated from my wife and children.

But this time the long trip was more than a flight of several thousand miles from North America to South Africa . . . more than a routine overseas hop. I was on my way home to the place of my earliest and happiest memories and to a family who cared deeply about me as a husband and father and son – who valued me as a person. To them I wasn't just Gary Player, world-hopping golf machine, but a human being with feelings and needs. My achievement at St. Louis would mean a lot more when I could share it with them.

Reflections on my childhood are stained deeply by painful memories of struggle and near-poverty. For thirty-one years my father, Harry Audley Player, had worked twelve to fourteen hours a day ten thousand feet underground in the Robinson Deep and Crown Gold Mines near Johannesburg. His top earnings during that time reached only about $450 a month, but the average hovered at around $300 – not much money for raising a family even in those days.

Because of the untimely death of his father, Dad left school after only four or five years to help support his mother and brothers and sisters. Those years of hard work on the farm deprived him of the opportunity to get any more formal education, but later as a husband and father he struggled hard to succeed and provide adequately for our family. And he did, but it took a lot of sweat and bone-breaking work.

My mother, Muriel Player, was a gentle and loving woman, a stickler for discipline and good manners, and very giving of herself. One of the earliest memories I have is of her helping Dad night after night when he was studying for the examination to become a mine captain. Mother was quite well educated, and with her support and an enormous amount of self-determination and discipline Dad passed those tests and received his promotion. As a result his take-home pay jumped almost

*Gary with his father, Harry Audley Player, at Zonnehoeve Plaas, Gary's home just outside Johannesburg. The elder Player's trademark, his infectious booming laugh, has earned him permanent nickname of "Laughing Harry".*

$100 a month. We thought we were rich.

Mother died of cancer at forty-four years of age when I was only eight. Her untimely death after four or five futile operations

*Gary's brother, Ian Player, is now Chief Game Conservator for Zululand's 500,000 acres of parks and game reserves with over 1 million game animals. His dedicated efforts to protect the wilderness and wildlife of the world were rewarded recently when he was named Conservationist of the Year by Game Conservation International.*

left a black emptiness in my young life. Suddenly, it seemed everything had turned upside down, and I ached with loneliness. But she left an imprint on me during those few short years that has never been erased. From her I began to understand the importance of courtesy and thoughtfulness for others and what it means to have faith in God as a blueprint for life. Each night Mother knelt beside my bed and listened to my prayers, helping me to understand that there is a God who loves us and who cares about what happens to people everywhere. These ideas and beliefs penetrated deeply into my consciousness, and even today, so many years later, they are inescapable. Courtesy, discipline, faith, love a rich heritage for a young boy!

When Mother died, my thirteen-year-old sister, Wilma, my brother, Ian, who was sixteen, and I experienced some dreadfully lonely times. But in spite of his own grief, my father put his arms around our family and held us all together with a strong feeling of love that persists to this day. After two or three years Dad remarried, and my stepmother is still very much a part of the family circle.

Dad is a big man who bears a strong resemblance to Wallace Beery (others have compared him to Victor McLaughlin, another actor of a past era). During my boyhood Dad tipped the scales at over two hundred pounds and seemed much taller than 6ft. 1in. A bluff and hearty person, he has an infectious, booming laugh that has long been a distinctive trademark. In fact, the nickname 'Laughing Harry' remains with him to this day.

When I was a young boy, Dad always had time for me, even after a backbreaking and exhausting day in the mine. And during the years that have followed we've had as fine a relationship as any father and son could possibly experience. He has been a great help to me all my life, and today, although he is seventy-four, we are as close as when I was eight.

One of the hardest things for me in the first years after my mother's death was the time before and after school. Just going to school meant leaving the house at six in the morning and bouncing along in two different buses for almost thirty miles. And then it would be nearly dark before I'd arrive home in the evening – to an empty house. Wilma had taken a job to help with expenses and Ian was away serving in the army. So, night after night, I waited alone in the dark on a bench in front of the house for Dad and Wilma to get home.

It's interesting, though, that I haven't the slightest recollection of feeling sorry for myself through any of those difficult years when I was alone so much. Probably that's because, even as a young boy, I had the idea drilled into me that strength of character comes from meeting and conquering adversity. It's not circumstances – good or bad – that make or break us, but how we handle and react to them.

More than anyone else Dad helped me recognize the importance of thinking creatively and positively as the first step in meeting the challenges of life. He would never make excuses or accept them. While Dad had a very tender heart, he knew it was absolutely necessary that I learn this lesson even if he had to be gruff at times. And he was.

I remember a conversation we had one day when I was still a teenager but had turned professional. I said, 'Gee, Dad, I'm too small. I don't think I'll ever become a champion.'

His sharp reply cut deeply into my mind and set me on a course I've tried to be faithful to ever since. 'Nonsense, it all depends on the guts you have. It's what's inside of you that matters, not what's on the outside.'

# 3 Grapevines and grit

*There's no room for can't in this life.*

'Ian, I just can't make it. I can't go on.' Heaving and gasping for breath, I caved in and sank to the ground. My lungs felt as if they would burst and sweat trickled off my body and formed little puddles in the dust.

Without any warning Ian yanked me to my feet and cuffed me on the side of the head. 'What do you mean you can't make it, man?' he exploded, his face flushed red and contorted with anger. 'You can do anything you want to. Remember that. There's no room for can't in this life.'

We were running together on a five-mile course Ian had laid out. And even though I was only about eight or nine at the time, he showed no mercy and always pressed me to the limit. His anger really scared me. I'll never know how I did it, but even though my feet felt like they were weighted down with lead and my leg muscles were knotted with pain, I ran the rest of that five miles without stopping for anything. Believe me, I was cured of ever threatening to quit in front of Ian again.

Persevere . . . never say can't . . . never give up. This fervid spirit saturated Ian's life even as a boy. He had suffered for years with a bad knee that put him in the hospital several times for operations and treatment. But through iron-willed determination and rigorous exercise he conquered the handicap so that even with his bad knee I couldn't keep up with him. Ian just refused to accept failure in any form.

Not long after that five-mile run incident, Ian quit school

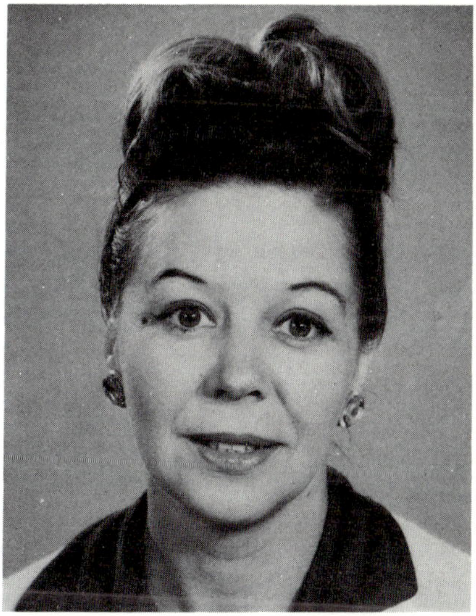

*Wilma Player Jacobs, Gary's sister, helped support the family after their mother's tragic death from cancer when Gary was eight; today she serves as Gary's secretary. Ian was then serving in the army, and Gary's father did back-breaking work as a goldminer.*

and joined the army, even though he was just within a few months of getting his diploma. World War II had been raging across Europe for several years, and, although only sixteen, Ian believed it was his duty to serve South Africa and the Allied cause in defence of freedom. Throughout his tour of duty he fought with an armoured division in Italy. Ian's record indicates that he gave a good account of himself, enduring the rigours and horrors of war and fighting alongside men much older and tougher than he.

Several years after the war Ian became a ranger with the Natal Parks Board. Today he is Chief Game Conservator for Zululand's five hundred thousand acres of parks and game reserves with over one million game animals. He has become known and respected around the world as a dedicated conservationist and saviour of the almost extinct white rhino. His life now is motivated by a consuming passion to protect the wilderness and wildlife of the world from the senseless ravages of man's greed and thoughtlessness. The rape of our natural resources is one of the great tragedies of what has passed for progress over the last fifty years. We were especially proud of Ian when his efforts were recognized and rewarded by Game Conservation International and he was named Conservationist of the Year.

In recent years Ian has launched a very innovative project called Wilderness Leadership School. Under this programme boys from England, Australia, and America, as well as from several other countries, visit South Africa and actually live in the bush for a time under supervision of the game wardens. The purpose of the school is to bring man to man, man to the soil, and man to God.

I am greatly in debt to my brother for teaching me at a very early age to be independent and to look out for myself. At the time, of course, I didn't begin to realize just how important this was, and some of the lessons he insisted I learn seemed unnecessarily hard. But that early training has made a tremendous difference in the shaping and development of my own life and attitudes.

There are a great many incidents out of my childhood and my relationship with Ian that are unforgettable. One summer in particular, when I was around seven or eight, stands out in bold relief in my memory. We had just moved into a new house at the mine, and there was a huge and lush grapevine loaded down with the juicy purple fruit just outside our door. The idea of having grapes in our own yard was a real treat for me, and I felt very protective of them. I considered the vine to be my own little piece of private property. One afternoon I caught several of the neighbourhood boys scrambling around in the upper branches. I ran up and proceeded to order them off the place in rather haughty fashion. They just looked at each other and then down at me. Nobody said a word, but one of the biggest boys dropped to the ground, snatched a large bunch of ripe grapes from the vine, and jammed it right into my face . . . squish!

Mad and humiliated, with grape juice in my hair and dripping from my chin, I ran crying to Ian. After I had sputtered and sobbed through my story, he plunked me down hard in a chair, looked me right in the eye, and said, 'Look now, you've got to learn to fight your own battles. Don't come running to me; stand up for yourself.'

At the time I was outraged with Ian's seemingly unsympathetic and harsh attitude. Nevertheless his words made a vivid and lasting impression on me. I began to understand the futility of running away and crying when the going gets rough or you don't get your way. It doesn't do a bit of good to gripe and complain about the adversities of life. Problems won't go away, either, by trying to ignore them. They must be confronted head-on.

A day or so after my grapevine lesson Ian tied a long rope to the highest limb of a tall tree in our yard. The rope must have been twenty-five or thirty feet long. Calling me out to see it, he said, 'Now look, if you want to be able to defend yourself, climb that rope clear to the top every day and get strong.' Every day after that I would pull and tug my way up through the branches to the top of that rope and then ease down slowly until my feet touched the ground again. The daily routine of rope climbing built strength into the muscles of my arms and shoulders. As I felt those muscles develop and gain strength, self-confidence seemed to energize every cell in my body with determination to achieve. Even today at age thirty-eight I can scramble up and down a rope with the same agility I had at nine or ten.

Ian also taught me to box and put me on a rigorous programme of weight-lifting and pushups. My day-to-day routine of practice never varied a bit, and I'm certain that it was this early training that instilled in me a great love for many different sports. There were times, of course, that I deeply resented this strict regimen of exercise and discipline, but even then I was beginning to feel the pride that comes with achievement. The electricity of competition generated sparks that would not be quenched. During my eleven years at King Edward VII School I earned letters in rugby and cricket, ran the 110-metre high and low hurdles, competed in swimming meets, and excelled in springboard diving. Athletics filled my mind almost to the exclusion of everything else. My small size didn't slow me down a bit nor blunt my competitive urge. In fact, when it came time to play or compete, I was as high-spirited and restless to get into action as a race horse at the starting gate.

It was during those school years that I began to understand the importance of discipline as an indispensable quality of success in any effort. My father and brother were indefatigable disciplinarians, demanding the last ounce of effort as the price for succeeding. And the teachers at King Edward School wouldn't put up with sloppiness in either our appearance or actions. Involvement in school sports activities was never just an option. If we didn't happen to be participating in a particular event, we were expected to be in the stands cheering for our classmates. There wasn't any room for the type of person who was satisfied to sit idly on the sidelines and watch everyone else perform. No one could get by just being a spectator.

But the discipline I responded to as a child was always tempered with love. Even while Dad and Ian were insisting on practice, practice, practice, and were demanding the ultimate in effort, I knew they loved me. Ours was a demonstrative family; no one shied away from authentic expressions of love and affection. And at the same time my teachers at school were always careful to balance their insistence on excellence with warmhearted assurance that they really cared for us as people.

Since then I've come to understand that discipline without love is dreadfully sterile and even cruel, and love without discipline produces softness and weakness, physically and morally. I believe strongly that these are the two poles around which our lives must revolve if we are to be whole and responsible human beings. Without discipline and love, we'd have a tough time surviving at all.

Those two qualities, discipline and love . . . the 'never-say-can't' attitude . . . pushed me beyond the boundaries of my little boy loneliness into the teenage world of competitive sports.

# 4 My growing obsession

*Even the birds and squirrels became old friends . . .*

Ian had whittled my first golf club from a stick and taught me a little bit about how to swing it. And my father was a 2-handicap golfer so it was only natural that I developed an early interest in the game. Even now I can remember the first time Dad took me out onto the course with him. Much to his surprise and mine, I managed to par three holes in a row. It was probably beginner's luck although my being extremely well co-ordinated certainly must have helped.

But the real clincher came when I caught my first glimpse of pretty Vivienne Verwey, whose father was the golf professional at Virginia Park Golf Course. I was attracted to her like a nail to a magnet. And when I saw her the second time I said to my stepbrother, somewhat brashly, 'Christopher, you know I'm going to marry that girl some day.' Imagine! I was only fourteen years old and she was thirteen, but that didn't intimidate me at all. There's no doubt that my feelings for her had a lot to do with my growing obsession with golf. Vivienne worked part-time in the pro shop helping her father by selling supplies and equipment so I started hanging around the club most of the time. Whenever anyone wanted golf tees or balls, I'd offer to run in and get them just for the chance to talk to Vivienne.

Happily, she felt the same way I did and it wasn't long before we were going steady. That was all the inspiration I needed to work really hard at golf. Mr. Verwey drilled me on the basics of the swing until the action seemed as natural as walking.

*At fifteen Gary was already practising 8 to 10 hours a day and dreaming of becoming a professional golfer.*

*His hopes were severely dashed later that year when he suffered a broken neck in a foolish accident and was forced into a painful period of inactivity that lasted well past his 16th birthday.*

His help and encouragement fired my determination, and I practised eight to ten hours every day as if my life depended on it.

Even then the dream of becoming a professional golfer began to take shape in my mind, driving me to greater effort. Being a natural athlete was a great asset and the hundreds of hours spent lifting weights, doing pushups, and pulling myself up the rope in the tree paid off. My wrist, arm, and shoulder muscles were already well developed and responded immediately to my almost fanatical concentration.

Several months later, when I was fifteen, a foolish kid stunt brought my budding golf career to a skidding halt. A gang of boys at school had taken over one side of the football field and wouldn't let anyone else walk through or cross on that side of the field. One day a couple of my friends and I decided to challenge them. Bolstered up by the support of the other kids, we ambled right into their private domain, and they jumped us. Naturally, that was exactly what we wanted. Fists began to fly and it wasn't long before we were locked together in a regular free-for-all.

It was a great scrap, and as I remember it, I think we fought to a draw. And then a funny thing happened. When the fight was over, we got to laughing about what had taken place and all of us became good friends.

A few days later we were walking together by a big compost pit near the school and one of the fellows suggested that it might be fun to run and jump or dive into the pit. As with boys from the beginning of time, we had gotten bored and craved some new form of excitement. I guess you might say we were the South African version of Tom Sawyer and Huckleberry Finn. The pit was filled with dried leaves and decomposed grass, making what appeared to be a soft cushion. When it was my turn, I took a good long run and dived head first right into the pit just as I would off a diving board. Crashing through the layers of leaves and grass, I hit the bottom with terrific force – crunch! The impact broke my neck and knocked me out cold.

Obviously, this foolish incident put an end to any kind of sports participation. No golf practice or weight-lifting or swimming – nothing. This was a painful time of inactivity, and I chafed with impatience to get back on the golf course just as soon as possible. My fifteen-year-old world with its grandiose plans and dreams had caved in, and there was nothing to do but wait it out. Time dragged interminably. The days seemed endless, but I continued to dream and visualize Gary Player striding confidently along fairways . . . holing long and difficult putts . . . winning tournaments around the world to the applause of appreciative galleries.

I was well past my sixteenth birthday before I could play again. It felt good to be back on the golf course, and for the next two years I spent every day playing and practising under the watchful eye and expert guidance of Mr. Verwey. Besides playing regular rounds I spent hours on the driving range, working diligently with each club, striving for pinpoint accuracy as well as distance. Like so many golfers, I had a problem shifting my weight to the left foot on the downswing. Executing this move properly adds considerable distance, and I worked hard to perfect it. Then from the driving range I would move on to the practice green and concentrate on my putting. I knew that the professional spends as much time there as on the practice tee. As I putted I would visualize playing in a major tournament and say to myself, 'Gary, you need this one to win.' Unfortunately, I didn't 'win' all that often, but I kept trying.

Virginia Park Golf Course became a second home for me. Every inch of the fairways and greens was familiar, and I knew the yardage to every bush and tree. Even the birds and squirrels became old friends.

These were long years of painful struggle, of muscle-stretching work, of intense concentration. Everything and everyone else in my life but Vivienne took second place to golf, and I'm sure there were times when she felt insecure and neglected. But I was determined to become good enough to play professional golf – and not just play, but win. I visualized playing first on the South African tour and then on those exotic faraway courses in America and England and Australia that I had read about – places I'd never been. But I would go someday, of that I was certain. Nothing else would satisfy me.

# 5 A penny-pinching time

*My world was getting bigger.*

When in 1953 at eighteen years of age I turned professional, there were more people who believed I'd never make it than thought I would. But the sceptics and those who joked about my chances only succeeded in goading me to greater effort. By this time Virginia Park had become a first home for me as I had moved in with the Verweys and could spend even more time practising – and, incidentally, with Vivienne. My dream of becoming a golf professional had actually materialized. I was now an $80-a-month assistant pro, and it was an exhilarating feeling!

My family and the Verweys had great confidence in me, but the local sportswriters insisted I'd never make it big because of my swing. In a way they were right; I didn't have a very good one then.

(But, what really makes a good golf swing? I don't believe there is any one answer to that question because golf swings vary so much even among the top professionals. Actually, you can select ten of the best players who ever lived, and they'll all swing the club differently. And my early hero, South African Bobby Locke, probably had one of the most awkward swings in the history of professional golf.)

I practised at least eight hours a day. At the time Virginia Park was open for play only on weekends, so the course was clear the rest of the time for practice and giving lessons.

Teaching proved a real test of my ability, but I enjoyed it

*Early in Gary's professional career he was assistant pro at Johannesburg's Killarney Golf Club. Members' generosity helped make possible Gary's first foreign tour. In this photograph Gary is still wearing his school (Honors) tie.*

*Spectators appraise Gary's form as he makes a chip shot at Kensington, Johannesburg, shortly after joining the pro tour.*

thoroughly and it helped a great deal in improving my own game. One of the first lessons I ever gave was to a fellow named Natie Voight. I'll never forget either him or his name. The cost of the lesson was only $1.50, but when we finished, he gave me a $3.00 tip. In all probability this was little more than a routine gesture for Natie Voight, but it certainly had a salutary effect on my spirits giving me just the ego-boost I needed at the time.

I had looked forward eagerly for many years to the opportunity of playing on the South African tour. After qualifying I made plans to enter every tournament possible. In order to have the money I needed for the first year, my father put his faith in me on the line and floated a bank loan.

To economize I played with used golf balls, and my clothes were pretty shabby even though they were the best I had. In fact, I was so embarrassed by my appearance that I borrowed a pair of pants from Vivienne's brother, Bob Verwey, when I was invited to play an exhibition match with Peter Thompson and Bobby Locke. Unfortunately, Bob weighed fifty pounds more than I did so it required an enormous amount of ingenuity even to get those pants to stay up. We managed to take up most of the slack with a series of gathers and tucks around the waist. Then to conceal the makeshift patch job I wore a heavy knit sweater which drooped down well below the waist and over the seat of my pants. It must have made quite a comical sight. Of one thing I am sure – it was hot. And though salty perspiration soaked my clothing, I didn't dare take that sweater off.

My feelings on the tour were a strange mixture of excitement, self-confidence and apprehension. The opportunity to play constituted the fulfilment of my boyhood dreams, and I was determined to make good. Although the only gallery that stayed with me during a tournament was my family, it's a good thing they did. Their belief in me supplied the confidence and support I desperately needed. Believe me, it went a long way toward helping me overcome the discouragement I felt when I'd return home between tournaments and hear comments from several members of my home club who freely expressed doubts that I would ever make it big. It seemed that I not only had my opponents on the course to face but also the doubters.

Much to my satisfaction and to the amazement of some, when the statistics were all in, I finished the tour in the top twelve. It was a particular thrill to capture second place in a tournament won by Bobby Locke.

During my early teenage years Bobby Locke had fired the imagination of every young South African golfer. His career was meteoric. Four times winner of the British Open and an impressive assortment of other major tournaments, Locke also distinguished himself by earning second place on the United States tour money list in 1947 and fourth in 1948. While Locke's swing was considered by some to be rather odd and quite awkward, he was a devastating chipper and putter – probably one of the finest in the history of golf.

I considered it a great honour to finish second to Locke in the tournament sponsored by the South African Tuberculosis Association and played at Wanderers Golf Club in Johannesburg. During the final round I got the biggest thrill of the entire year at the 9th hole. Executed from roughly forty-five yards from the green, my wedge shot arced beautifully, headed straight for the pin, and rolled right into the hole. The cheer that went up from the gallery made up for all the hard work and occasional disappointments that were so much a part of that first year.

But it was especially exciting to take home the second-place prize money – approximately six hundred dollars. There was just enough to buy my first automobile – a little green Austin with a sun top which opened and closed and an open muffler that clattered loud enough to completely satisfy my teenage taste. That little car was the pride of my life, and I polished it almost to the point of rubbing the paint thin. But there was just one problem, and it was a big one. I didn't have enough money left to buy petrol – at least as much as I wanted to use – so I ran out with monotonous regularity. This really irked my father and Mr. Verwey. Just the same, time after time they grudgingly pushed me to the nearest garage, where I always vowed it wouldn't happen again. But it did.

1953 and 1954 were satisfying years. I was doing what I enjoyed most, and my golf game improved steadily. But 1955, the year of my first tournament win on the South African tour, was the turning point. Coming just two years after I had turned professional, that first win – the East Rand Open at Benoni Country Club in Benoni, a suburb of Johannesburg – will always stand out as one of the most exciting events in my life. Since then I've won approximately one hundred tournaments in many different countries, but my pulse still quickens at the memory of that first one.

At the presentation I received the usual congratulations from other players and the tournament officials, but the thing that meant the most to me occurred when my father walked up and extended his hand man-to-man. That handshake and the look of pride in his eyes was one of the most moving experiences in my life. At that moment I felt I was a man.

By this time I had left Virginia Park for the assistant pro job at Killarney Golf Club, also in Johannesburg. And it was the generosity of Killarney members that made it possible for me to go on my first foreign tour. They took up a collection which netted one hundred and seventy-five rand – about five hundred dollars then. This, plus an overdraft at the bank, arranged for by my father to cover plane fare, was enough, we figured, to keep me going for about two months.

With my first tournament win behind me, now came my first airplane ride, my first trip far away from home, my first experience in a foreign country. In fact, 1955 was a whole year of firsts for me. I was as excited as a boy on his first date – and about as confident. It would have been impossible to predict the outcome, but one thing was certain as sunrise – I intended to enjoy every bit of it.

Following the goodbyes – and they were quite emotional – I climbed aboard the plane. Johannesburg faded into the distance, and even though my stomach was churning, my mind flipped ahead toward the first stop: Cairo, Egypt, capital city of the colourful and fabled land that has played such a important part in world history. It was to be the site of the Egyptian Match Play Championship. Four other South African golfers were on the plane that day – Harry Middleton, Harold Henning, Brian Wilkes, and Doug Evans – and we made up an excited fivesome.

The Gezira Sporting Club, where the tournament was played, just has to be one of the most beautiful courses I have ever seen. I remember my amazement in learning that at night the course, located right on the banks of the Nile River, was actually flooded with water from the Nile. No wonder the fairways and landscape were so lush and green.

Some of the finest Egyptian golfers were entered in this event, including Mohammed Dusse, who still plays quite regularly in the World Cup. But as the days passed, Harold Henning and I successfully eliminated all of them, so the two of us were matched against each other in the final round. The competition waxed hot as the Egyptian sun, and we seesawed back and forth, but I won the round and captured the title.

Winning the Egyptian Match Play brought me first-prize money of three hundred pounds, about nine hundred dollars. Now if I handled the money carefully, there would be enough to extend the tour by at least another two months.

Before leaving Egypt, though, we did the usual sight-seeing – the pyramids, the sphinx, and even a jolting camel ride across the hot sand. I'm sure the Egyptians thought we were a pretty zany lot. But my world, which up to this point had been quite limited, seemed to explode with each new experience. This first taste of a strange culture, of making new friends in a foreign country, added fuel to the spark of ambition that has motivated me ever since. My mind and emotions soaked it all up, until it seemed that every cell and nerve in my body responded with almost frightening intensity.

Flushed with that first taste of victory in Egypt, I headed for England and the British golf circuit. Practice and tournament play consumed every moment; nothing else mattered. It was a thrill, and even awesome, to compete on some of the courses I had heard so much about. Old and historic St. Andrews, the golfer's mecca, held a special fascination for me. The rich heritage of golf saturated the air . . . and I breathed deeply.

With careful planning my original stake and the Egyptian winnings lasted a full and excitement-packed five months. Believe me, it was a penny-pinching time! Cutting every corner possible, I was downright miserly. To avoid the extravagance of tipping the porters I'd trudge from station to train and from train to station lugging my suitcase and player satchel under one arm and dragging my golf bag along with the other. I literally wore the bottom off the bag on that tour. Quite a funny sight, I'm sure, but it was all deadly serious business to me.

After working through my money until there was just barely enough left for a plane ticket home, I headed south for Johannesburg. Homesick for Vivienne and my family, and eager to be home, I knew something momentous had happened to me

*Gary on his first trip to England. It cost him 17/6 (17 shillings and sixpence) at this lodging house for bed and a breakfast of fried bread and tomato.*

during those five months: I had ventured my first tentative steps toward becoming a world golfer. Since then my travels have taken me more than four million miles, and I've played most of the world's finest courses before sympathetic and enthusiastic galleries. But 1955 . . . Egypt and England . . . was when and where it all began.

# 6 Vivid dreams

*Buy the wedding dress*!

Vivienne and I had been going together steadily for six years and wanted desperately to get married, but there just wasn't enough money. We were broke all the time, but before going to Melbourne, Australia, in 1956 I said, 'Look, I'm going to play in the Ampol tournament. If I win, we'll get married right away. I don't know whether I stand much of a chance, but I'm really going to try. There are a lot of good American, British, and Australian players entered in the tournament.'

What stronger motivation could a young man in love have! I played through the opening rounds of the Ampol tournament, which was held in conjunction with the Olympic games, obsessed with the desire to win and was leading with just one round to go. But play on the final day was washed out by a torrential rain that flooded the course so I had to sit around and wait. The tension was electric, and my nerves were as taut as a bow string. But it was dry enough for us to go the next day, and I played exceptionally well on that final round, finishing with a safe seven-stroke lead. There are just no words adequate to describe my excitement as I walked, or floated, away from that last hole.

First-prize money was five thousand pounds, about fourteen thousand dollars – enough to get married in style, with enough left over to live comfortably for awhile. I headed straight for the telegraph office from the golf course to send Vivienne a cable: 'Buy the wedding dress. We'll be married immediately.'

Undoubtedly that plane from Melbourne to Johannesburg flew at its usual fast rate of speed, but it just seemed that we would never get there. Time dragged by at a snail's pace, and my stomach knotted with anticipation. Never did the huge gold dumps of Johannesburg sparkle so brilliantly or look so beautiful as when we finally descended for our landing. And never had Vivienne looked more radiant.

Vivienne and I were married on the afternoon of January 19, 1957, at Central Hall Methodist Church in Johannesburg by Vivienne's pastor, the Reverend Joseph B. Webb. Our friends and relatives filled the beautifully decorated church. Vivienne's matron of honour was Bob Charles' wife, Verity, and my brother Ian served as best man. There was no question in my mind that Vivienne was the most beautiful bride ever to walk down an aisle.

Following the wedding reception we drove to Scotsborogh, a delightful and scenic resort on the south coast, for a ten-day honeymoon. Frequently I'm asked if we played golf on our honeymoon. Yes, of course. Vivienne was a two-handicap golfer at the time and enjoyed playing as much as I did. So we played almost every day. In fact, I played nine holes in the morning before our wedding.

As you can imagine, I have a warm place in my heart for Australia. Altogether I've been there fifteen times, and Australia has been very good to me. I won the PGA in 1957; the Australian Open in 1958, 1962, 1963, 1965, 1969, 1970 – a record for one golfer; and the Australian Wills Masters in 1968. But that first Ampol win in 1956 ranks high in contention as the biggest thrill of them all. I'm indebted to Norman Von Nida, an Australian golfer, for my invitation to play in the Ampol.

(*Opposite page*) *Gary and bride, the former Vivienne Verwey, had been sweethearts from their early teens when they met at Virginia Park Golf Course where Vivienne's father was the club professional. The wedding took place January 19, 1957, at the Central Hall Methodist Church in Johannesburg, after Gary won the £5000 first prize money at the Australian Ampol tournament.*

*Vivienne and Gary. Vivienne, who shares Gary's love for golf, was a two-handicap golfer at the time of their wedding, and the two played golf almost every day during their honeymoon.*

Earlier in 1956 I had entered the Dunlop tournament at Sunningdale Golf Club in Surrey, England. My playing partner was Arthur Lees, the Sunningdale professional, and the tournament developed into a duel between us. An exceptionally good match player and a great competitor, Arthur had never been beaten on his home course.

The Dunlop was a five-round tournament, and I won it with a total score of 338: 70, 64, 64, 68, 72, a world record for five rounds that still stands, although it has been equalled once by Arnold Palmer at a Bob Hope Classic.

*Gary in 1956 had just taken his first steps toward becoming a world golfer. His first big win in England came when he scored 70-64-64-68-72 for the 90-hole Dunlop Masters, setting a world record that is still unbroken.*

It was during the Dunlop that Norman Von Nida came up to me and said, 'Son, you've really got it.' I asked, 'What is *it*?' And he responded, 'Well, nobody can define *it*, but you've got it. I'm going to arrange an invitation for you to go to Australia and play in the Ampol.' He did, so I have Norman to thank for a chance to play in the event that made my marriage to Vivienne possible at that time.

*Mr Beharrel of Dunlop's presents Gary with his first-place trophy as winner of the 1956 Dunlop Masters.*

In more ways than one, 1956 holds the distinction of being an extremely eventful year in my life. In addition to the Ampol I won my first South African Open Championship, played at Durban Country Club, one of my favourite courses. Winning the Open and earning the National Open Championship title gave me tremendous satisfaction because of my disappointing showing the year before in not even qualifying. Between 1956 and 1972 I was successful in winning this title a total of eight times – a record I'm proud to hold. Also it was in 1956 that I was first voted South African Sportsman of the Year. Since then I have received this coveted honour five more times.

But it was the exhilaration of travel . . . of playing golf in foreign countries . . . of winning tournaments in different time zones that fired my imagination. As a boy in Johannesburg, I had dreamed about England, Japan, the United States, Australia; but they were fantasy places at the end of some distant rainbow – out of reach for a South African miner's son. Then, as a teenage golfer, grimly practising my heart out at Virginia Park, I would let my mind drift and my imagination take over. The pictures of playing in faraway places were so vivid it was almost impossible not to believe they were real. These were the days I first dreamed of becoming the best golfer in the world – not just in South Africa or England or the United States, but in the world.

By the end of 1956, playing golf and winning tournaments in England, Egypt, Australia, as well as in South Africa, were dreams come true. Travel to those different countries was personally enriching, and I grew up a lot. The goal of becoming the top world golfer became a mounting obsession.

Then in 1957 Clifford Roberts, in response to a letter my father had written, gave me an invitation to the American Masters. This marked my first year on the United States tour. My horizons were expanding, and in the years to follow they were to include the whole world. Today I commute from Johannesburg to Japan or the United States with a regularity almost comparable to that of a suburban businessman catching the local to downtown New York or Chicago or London.

To me, this is the test of a dedicated professional golfer. It is one thing to score well in your home country under familiar conditions, but to face up to the adversities of foreign play is the mark of a champion. Time changes, unusual food, different grasses, sand greens, poorly kept fairways, an unfamiliar atmosphere, foreign languages, mediocre accommodations, changes of climate and altitude – all of these offer a severe test to a player, physically and emotionally. To strive to become the best in any profession demands intense personal sacrifice and effort. And for me it means being away from my wife and children, aching with homesickness, travelling and living under all sorts of conditions in a wide variety of climates, playing golf from Johannesburg to St. Andrews . . . from Augusta to Tokyo . . . from Madrid to Melbourne . . . from Pebble Beach to Rio de Janeiro.

But perhaps the greatest reward I receive from travelling and playing golf in so many countries is the opportunity to make and form solid friendships with people of different races and cultures. I firmly believe that the suspicion and hatred which is so much a part of life today could be dispelled if we would really get to know one another. Knowing creates understanding.

And everywhere I go I have good friends. People are important to me. I think a man is rich not because he has money but because he has friends. One of life's great miracles is that God has made us all different. We aren't gingerbread people stamped out by some cosmic cookie cutter. Our fingerprints, faces, personalities, are unique to each of us. We're each one of a kind.

According to Shakespeare, the world's a stage and everybody plays a part. And I believe my part is to continue toward my goal of being the top world-class golfer . . . of enjoying my friends and associates in many different countries . . . of being an ambassador of goodwill and spreading feelings of love and peace wherever I go – in the galleries along the fairways and greens, in hotel lobbies, everywhere. It is my prayer that God will use me to mirror his love and goodwill in every part of my personal and professional life. I really feel I'm a salesman for God when I travel.

# 7 Grand slam

*I decided to attack.*

'You have the game to win this tournament. You can get in there and win it if you just make yourself realize that.' This encouraging send-off came from John Jacobs, an outstanding professional golfer and teacher, before the opening round of the 1959 British Open at Muirfield Golf Links in Muirfield, Scotland. If I could win this one, it would give me the first leg of golf's Grand Slam, and I wanted it desperately.

I had arrived at Muirfield ten days early in order to have plenty of time for practice. The winds there are very tricky, and I wanted to be thoroughly familiar with the course, working out carefully the distances involved in each hole and the clubs that would be required in any possible situation.

My game at this time was really quite smooth. The year before I had succeeded in overcoming three faults that had plagued me from the beginning: a wide stance, a flat arc, and a hooker's hand action. Now my swing was more compact and rhythmic than it had ever been before. Even though still only twenty-three years old and short on professional experience, I was ready and eager to win this tournament, a prestigious and historic event. The British Open was born in 1860 at Prestwick Golf Club on the west coast of Scotland, and Willie Park had captured the first title. Now, ninety-nine years later, I wanted above everything else to see the name of Gary Player in the winner's spot.

But as we came up to the last day of play, I lagged eight

strokes behind the leaders, Flory Van Donck of Belgium and Fred Bullock of Great Britain. Even so, the night before in a conversation with Pat Matthews I had said, 'Pat, I'm eight strokes behind, but I really feel I'm going to win this tournament tomorrow.' In those days we played 36 holes on the last round, and I set out to fulfil that prophecy of the night before, beginning my charge right from the first hole. I had a super round until the last hole, where I needed a par 4 for a 66. On my tee shot I drove into a large bunker on the left of the fairway, leaving me no alternative but to hit safely back to the fairway. From there I used a 6-iron to the green, but the ball landed well short of the pin. Then I 3-putted for a 6, giving me a 68 for the round and a total score of 284 for the 72 holes. In all probability I had thrown away the championship, but there was really no way of knowing for sure because the leaders were playing two hours behind me. This meant a long and painful wait for the final results.

My nerves were taut, and it was impossible to sit still, so my friend George Blumberg and I paced up and down the 400-yard driveway by the clubhouse. Back and forth we went, but it didn't help at all. After a time I went back over to my hotel room and took a cold bath. This seemed to settle my nerves a bit, so George and I returned to the clubhouse, where George Gibson, secretary of the PGCA, took us to the top balcony to watch the last players come up to the 18th green.

When the final player holed out, it really hit me: I had won the British Open Championship – one of the four major championships in the world of golf. And I had beaten Flory Van Donck, a superb Belgian golfer, by two strokes.

This was one of the great moments in my life – a never-to-be-forgotten thrill, blunted only by the fact that my father, whose ambition it had been to see me win the British Open, was not there. But Vivienne and our three-month-old daughter, Jennifer, were there to share in the excitement.

And just to prove how excited I really was, I showed up at the award ceremonies a full half-hour ahead of time. Decked out in a milk white suit with a red and white striped tie, I sat and waited for everyone else to arrive. It's difficult now to isolate all of the thoughts that raced through my mind during that wait. But with the first leg of the big four behind, my thoughts turned to the remaining three. At that point it wasn't a question of whether or not it would happen, but when.

Arrival at Augusta National Golf Club in Georgia in the spring of 1961 for the American Masters marked my fourth year of competition in this tournament. And the best I had done so far was a tie for sixth place in 1960. Arnold Palmer, the defending champion, was the undisputed and popular favourite in 1961.

In fact, according to Alfred Wright in *Sports Illustrated* (April 17, 1961):

'When the winter tour began at Los Angeles last January, there was no one in sight to challenge Palmer's towering prestige. As if to confirm his stature, he quickly won three of the first eight tournaments. Player won only one. But as the tour reached Pensacola a month ago, Player was leading Palmer in official winnings by a few hundred dollars, and the rest of the field was somewhere off in nowhere. On the final round at Pensacola, the luck of the draw paired Palmer and Player in the same threesome, and although it was far from obvious at the time, the gallery was treated to the first chapter of what promises to be one of the most exciting duels in sports for a long time.

'On the final Sunday at Pensacola neither Palmer nor Player was leading the tournament and, as it turned out, neither won it. But whichever of these two finished ahead of the other would be the undisputed financial leader of the tour. Player immediately proved he was not in the least awed by the dramatic proximity of Palmer. He outplayed Palmer all around the course and finished with a tremendous 65 to Palmer's 71. Thereafter, until the Masters, Player gradually increased his lead over Palmer in winnings and added one more tournament victory at Miami. When they reached Augusta last week, together they had won 5 of the 13 tournaments to date.'

The stage was set for the 1961 Masters. Rain complicated action somewhat on opening day, but Arnold shot a 68, four under par, and I came in just one stroke behind with a 69. On the second day of competition I birdied 1, 9, 13, 15, and 18. In addition to the five birdies I had twelve pars and one bogey, giving me a score of 68. Arnold was playing behind me and completed his round with a 69.

On the third round I got off to a strong start with birdies on 1, 2, 6, and 8. Then I ran into bad trouble. On the 420-yard 9th hole a poor tee shot landed in the woods and presented me with a crucial choice: I could hit safely back to the fairway and then go for the green, a sure bogey; or I could attack. Since I had been hitting the ball well, it seemed smart to attack. Selecting a 4-wood, I hit out to the first fairway, slicing it sharply to the 9th green where it rolled to a stop a short distance from the edge. A carefully placed chip shot and one putt saved par.

My fortunes took a turn for the worse on the back nine when I bogied 11, 12, and 13. But birdies on 15 and 16 gave me a score of 69. Meanwhile Arnold had a tortuous round with a one-over-par 73. I now held a four-stroke lead.

A heavy rainstorm washed out the fourth round halfway through on Sunday so I had to sit it out until Monday. And it was pure agony! But we started on schedule the next day, and everything went smoothly for me on the front nine: I posted a 34. But disaster struck on the back nine when I bogied 10, double-bogied 13, and bogied 15 to finish the round with a two-over-par 74 and a total of 280 for the tournament. At this point Arnold, who was playing behind me, had a lead of one stroke, and he held onto it tenaciously until his final hole.

Vivienne and I watched Arnold play the last hole on television in Clifford Roberts' apartment. When we saw Palmer's tee shot zip right down the middle of the fairway, I thought it was all over. But a poor approach shot put him in a bunker, and it took him two more to get within fifteen feet of the cup. Now he was putting for a tie, and it looked as if we were headed for a playoff. But to my absolute amazement, Arnold missed that putt by inches and finished the round with a 281. The American Masters Championship was mine by one stroke.

It was very disturbing, though, when some sports writers insisted that my win came because Arnold Palmer threw it away on the last hole. After all, I'd been fairly secure with a four-shot lead until the 13th and then ran into trouble myself with a seven – followed by a six on 15. It was just that my difficulties started before Arnold's. And if a player is going to run into serious trouble at Augusta National Golf Course, it will happen on the back nine with its treacherous make-or-break quality. But I've always been grateful to *Sports Illustrated* for the fact that they gave me full credit for the win in their reporting of the tournament.

Now with this title added to my 1959 British Open win, I had arrived at the halfway mark toward the coveted Grand Slam.

Fortunately, there have been few really low points in my golf career, but July of 1962 is certainly a candidate for the cellar spot. Victory seemed as hard to grasp as a bead of mercury in the palm of your hand. It had been fifteen long months since I'd chalked up a tournament win, and to compound the misery, just the week before I had even failed to qualify for the last two rounds of the British Open. Missing the cut at Troon drove my spirits into a steep nose dive.

It is vitally important for a professional golfer to win, and I'm certainly no exception. But winning consistently, day after day, is virtually impossible in golf. For example, Jack Nicklaus may play in twenty-five major tournaments a year and actually win only five or six. And yet Jack is unquestionably a champion and one of the finest golfers in the history of the sport. This is precisely why I rate golf as the most difficult sport in the world.

By contrast, a top-class athlete in practically any other sport will win regularly while at his peak. But not so in golf; there are just too many variables. The golfer plays on different courses for each tournament. The grasses vary . . . one day the fairways play long, the next day short . . . at times they're wet and later they're dry . . . the greens may be fast on one round and slow on the next . . . bunkers have different textures of sand . . . one day the wind is blowing from the west, while the next day it may sweep in from the north or east. Then, too, the golfer's reflexes must respond with split-second timing. The margin for error is minimal. If the impact between the club-head and ball is off just two degrees, a shot may veer sixty yards either to the left or right two hundred and fifty yards down the fairway. And even the slightest variation in the speed of the swing can make a tremendous difference in your game.

These are conditions I know and accept, but to go fifteen months without a tournament win and to miss the cut at the British Open had really sapped my morale.

So upon my arrival at Aronimink Golf Club near Philadelphia to play in the forty-fourth PGA tournament, I confided to a friend my intense feelings of frustration and the desire to give it all up and return permanently to South Africa. Knowing, though, that, whatever my decision, this tournament came first, I settled down to practise and concentrate on my game. And a miraculous thing happened. I'ts hard to explain, but I described it this way in my earlier book entitled *Grand Slam Golf,* 'A fantastic change came over me. Here was a marvellous course, green and ripe, with lush fairways, dazzling white bunkers, holding greens, lovely trees everywhere. All my life I've loved trees. . . . The whole setting was peaceful and so sympathetic to me after the brutalities of Troon that I felt happy, relaxed, and invigorated.' Flooded with confidence and the conviction that I wasn't washed up at twenty-four, it was now up to me to prove it.

After posting a 72 for the first round, I came through with a 67 the next day to move into a three-way tie for second place with George Bayer and Cary Middlecoff. We all hovered just one shot off the lead.

My 69 on Saturday, giving me a three-round total of 208, moved me into the lead by two strokes. In the final round I held my lead solidly through the first thirteen holes and then Bob Goalby, my playing partner, made a strong challenge when he birdied 14 and 16, narrowing my lead to just one stroke. We both took a par on 17. On the 18th hole Bob's approach shot was inside of mine; he was in a very good position to birdie and move into a tie. When I missed a thirty-foot putt, it seemed inevitable that we'd have to settle for a tie that would take us into a playoff. But Goalby missed his putt by inches, and I holed mine to finish with a 287 – one stroke up on Goalby and three over Jack Nicklaus.

Those days at Aronimink completely revolutionized my outlook on the future. Confidence had been restored. I was a new person, and instead of thinking about retiring, my thoughts zeroed in on the United States Open. Now, only this tournament blocked my goal of capturing all four of the big ones. The Grand Slam was within reaching distance.

In 1963 the United States Open was played at the Country Club at Brookline, Massachusetts. After 72 holes, Julius Boros, Jackie Cupit, and Arnold Palmer were locked in a three-way tie. In the 18-hole playoff Julius Boros took the championship with a 70 to Cupit's 73 and Palmer's 76. That year I finished in eighth place.

The following year, 1964, when the Open took place at Congressional Country Club in Washington, D.C., I wasn't even in contention. Over two years had slipped by since my PGA victory. During this time I had won six tournaments and placed in the top ten 26 times, but my thoughts were concentrated on *one* tournament – the one tournament I must win to join Ben Hogan and Gene Sarazen in the 'big four' circle.

But in 1965 the United States Open win at Bellerive Country Club in St. Louis saw the fulfillment of my long-standing and vivid dream. The climb to the top had seemed endless and fraught with heartbreaking obstacles. The rarefied air at the pinnacle of the Grand Slam was heady, but the view of the future seemed far more brilliant than ever before.

# 8 The many faces of success

*Call Mr. Dunlop* !

I believe that Ben Hogan knows more about golf than any other man has ever known. He was the supreme master golfer. So one day while playing in the Brazilian Open in 1973 I decided to put through a long distance call to Mr. Hogan in Fort Worth, Texas, and ask him a question about the golf swing.

When the overseas operator got the call through and Mr. Hogan answered, I said, 'Mr. Hogan, this is Gary Player. Outside of you I figure I have practised harder than anyone else in the history of golf. I will understand if you do not care to answer, but I must ask if you'll allow me this one question about a golf swing.'

Everything was quiet for a moment or two and then Mr. Hogan said, 'Gary, who do you work for?' When I told him Dunlop, he replied, 'Well, call Mr. Dunlop.' And without another word he slammed the receiver down in my ear.

A similar thing happened to Ben Crenshaw when he called Mr. Hogan to ask him a question. In response to the query as to what kind of equipment he was using, Ben told him MacGregor. Whereupon Mr. Hogan said, 'Call Mr. MacGregor,' and hung up.

I guess the moral to these stories is that if you want to ask Mr. Hogan a question, you'd better tell him ahead of time that you are using Ben Hogan equipment. But the point I want to make here is that I think Ben Hogan is such a great golfer and is so knowledgeable that if instead of hanging up on me so abruptly he had said, 'Gary, why don't you come up here and we'll talk about it,' I would have done it. I'd gladly have flown from Brazil to Texas to spend an hour discussing the golf swing with him.

Why was Ben Hogan so successful? I realize, of course, that success has many faces, but among other things Mr. Hogan had complete dedication to golf throughout his long and brilliant career. He always knew exactly what to do and how to do it, and he did it when it mattered most. Ben Hogan's success came through hard work and consistent practice. He never gave up or was complacent. Complacency breeds failure in any area of life. The person who doesn't work hard, who gives up easily and quits, will never become a winner. A bulldog kind of tenacity is absolutely essential to success in any venture.

I recall just one time in my life when I quit trying on a golf course. This occurred during one of my first tournaments as a professional when I was only about seventeen years old. But the course was in dreadful condition, and no matter what I did, my putting game wouldn't come together. It seemed as if the further along I went the worse it got, so eventually I just gave up. And at that moment I was a failure.

Just four years ago I sent the tournament officials a letter of apology expressing my feelings of shame for having been so rude.

In addition to hard work and persistence I believe that a successful person is one who has his feelings under control. One thing is certain – the world of golf is no place for a flighty or temperamental person.

Whenever there is a discussion on temperament in the golf world, the name of Tommy Bolt is sure to come up. Sports-writers and golfers used to call him the even-tempered lad – always mad. Tommy was an exceptionally talented golfer, but if the slightest thing happened to upset him, he'd start to swear and throw clubs. Nevertheless, it's true he has won some tournaments. He took the United States Open Championship in 1958 when I placed second. But I believe he could have captured many more tournament titles if he had kept his temper under control.

One time at the Jackie Gleason tournament, when Bolt was watching Arnold Palmer, he said, 'You know, everybody criticizes me for throwing clubs. Arnold Palmer's wife, Winnie, was the greatest club retriever that ever lived. Only Arnold Palmer couldn't throw the clubs as well as I could, so he decided to become a good player.'

On another occasion Bolt ran into a streak of luck so bad that he took recourse in throwing clubs all over the place. As he sized up his approach shot to the green on the last hole, Tommy looked at his caddie and asked, 'Well, what do you think?'

'I think it's about a 2-iron,' the caddie replied.

'How many yards have we got?' Bolt asked as he took another look toward the green.

'About 120.'

'How can it possibly be a 2-iron?' Bolt demanded angrily.

'Well, that's the only club we've got left.'

I've never been absolutely certain that incident actually took place, but it's been reported for the truth on more than one occasion. At any rate, it is very much in character.

Bobby Locke was a golfer with an amazingly even temperament. He did everything quietly and in slow motion. It didn't make any difference whether he was playing in a tournament, driving a car, or changing his shoes in the locker room, Bobby moved slowly, but every motion had a purpose. He just refused to get upset about anything or rush around in a flurry. And I'm convinced that's one reason at least he was such an outstanding golfer.

And Jack Nicklaus is a marvel when it comes to temperament. In fact I think he has the most even disposition of any human being who's ever played golf. Even when Jack is hitting the ball poorly I've seen him come off the course with a 68. The secret is his ability always to remain calm and on an even keel. By keeping cool he's usually able to convert an almost disastrous or impossible situation into an asset. A man who can do that is a real champion – a truly successful man and a winner. Frequently I hear tournament golfers complain about a particular course, implying that conditions prevent them from playing as well as usual. This is nonsense. We all play the same holes. The true champion plays the game on any course and under all conditions without resorting to excuses.

I've tried hard to learn this lesson. And it's especially important since my own life-style is quite frantic because of the varied interests that absorb my time and energy. I try to keep in mind the words my sister, who is a very spiritual person, once handed me on a piece of paper: 'Jesus moves slowly so make sure you do.' I'll admit it's easy to get upset and rush around when the pressure is on, and sometimes I become very irritated and impatient when things don't move according to my timing. Unfortunately, the hyperactivity of our times is corroding our ability to live full and satisfying lives.

Another ingredient of success that I regard as exceptionally important is the art of thinking positively – of cultivating healthy attitudes. Dr. Norman Vincent Peale, the pastor of Marble Collegiate Church in New York City has influenced my life greatly through his book *The Power of Positive Thinking* and his sermons. I firmly believe that the way we think determines what we are and what we can be. When I'm on the tee, I try to concentrate my thoughts on the precise line I want my drive to take and the exact spot where it will roll to a stop on the fairway. Obviously, thinking . . . concentrating . . . visualizing can never take the place of tireless practice and the perfecting of one's skills. But mechanical skill without right attitudes and positive thoughts will never produce a winner.

Alfred Dyer, my regular caddie on the American tour, is a superb example of an optimistic and right-thinking person. Rabbit, a nickname which apparently described him best as a high jumping, 6ft. 6in. basketball player, has a marvellous disposition and is the best caddie I've ever had. Even though he has been out early in the morning checking pin placements and measuring yardage from sprinklers on the fairway to the front of the green, he always has a big smile and an encouraging word for me later in the day when I'm playing the round. And even when I'm not playing well, Rabbit keeps his head high and doesn't sulk; he knows I'm trying hard. Then after the round in the late afternoon if I want to go out to the practice tee and hit balls for an hour or so, he's right there with me. This is a great encouragement, and I really appreciate him as a caddie and as a person, but above all as a friend.

Developing the art of thinking positively is the best way I know to handle those times when everything may not be going just right. And there are plenty of those. I've had days out on the golf course when I worked hard and played well and still shot a 75. In such a depressing situation, it would be easy to really get down in the dumps and feel sorry for myself. So when this happens, I sit down with a pencil and paper and write out all the good things I have and enjoy: I am healthy and in good physical condition; I have a beautiful home . . . a wonderful wife . . . a loving and happy family . . . I'm doing the thing I like best – playing golf.

Before I know it my list of blessings is so long that I can't remember what caused my depression in the first place. A person's life graph can't reflect 'ups' all the time; everyone is bound to have some 'downs'. But the person who has a positive mental outlook . . . who visualizes good things happening . . . who expects the best, doesn't stay down very long. Perspective is regained rapidly and things begin to work out. The hardest thing for most people to learn in golf is to accept bad holes and then forget about them.

But I suppose that when I think about those qualities which to me at least are prerequisite to success in golf, and in all of life, the one that stands out the most is the ability to accept adversity – the ability to acknowledge and handle the apparent obstacles that can, if allowed to, bring defeat. I think it was during the 1961 Masters that Billy Graham, a man who has exerted a great influence in my life, said to me, 'You know, Gary, you must realize that to be able to accept things in adversity is a great test.' It is easy to be thankful for the good things that come our way in life. But it is quite another matter to thank God for the difficulties we encounter. And I do believe that success in any part of life comes only through the struggle to overcome the setbacks and hard things. I think it was President Harry Truman who said, 'I'm inclined to agree with Sir Francis Bacon that: The good things which belong to prosperity are to be wished for, but the good things that belong to adversity are to be admired.'

The will to succeed against adversity is what builds character and brings satisfaction and happiness. But it seems today that many people are looking for easy solutions – an easy way out. And there are those in increasing numbers who attempt to escape through alcohol or drugs. If I may say so, this is the supreme copout. It just doesn't work and only multiplies problems.

My life as a boy was very hard, and I missed terribly the love of my mother after her death. But I'm very grateful to my father and brother for helping me see even then that the great challenges and rewards come through overcoming and winning out over seeming handicaps.

During the early years of my golf career some people predicted that my small size would wipe out any chance of success. This just drove me to practise harder and exercise strenuously to develop and strengthen my muscles and body.

Even today the sports writers talk about '150 pound, 5ft. 7in. Gary Player' . . . 'the diminutive Black Knight from South Africa' . . . 'the gritty little man from Johannesburg.' But I never think of myself as a small person. If I'm playing with Jack Nicklaus, I don't look over at him and think, 'Gee, Jack is really big and strong.' This never enters my thinking because in my mind I'm just as big and strong as he is.

Occasionally you will hear someone describe a particular golf course as one strictly for the big fellows who are long hitters. I don't believe this. There's no such thing as a course just being good for the long hitter. Actually, the golf course is built for the man who can get the ball in the hole with the least number of strokes.

My good friend Chi Chi Rodriguez is a small man who has refused to let size be a handicap to his success as a professional golfer. He weighs only 125 pounds, but he has great speed and what I call suppleness of the hips. When Chi Chi swings, he really moves those hips into the ball and gets tremendous distance for such a tiny man. But even more important, he is an exceptionally kind person, vigorously competitive but still very sensitive to the feelings of other people.

As I travel regularly from country to country, I've come to know many of the world leaders in business, politics, and sports. Upon close examination they all seem to share one common trait: the will to overcome the adversities of life and turn them into authentic successes . . . the determination to win in spite of the reverses and handicaps that in one way or another come to all of us.

I remember the time my good friend and mentor George Blumberg a highly successful South African businessman and golfing enthusiast said to me 'Gary, I'm going to tell you something now I hope you will always remember. Popularity is something nonachievers try to substitute for achievement. All you must strive for is achievement, nothing else.' There's no question that in many ways this comment portrays in living colour my own outlook on life. But at the same time I think it is tremendously important that a person's drive for achievement and success be kept in proper perspective. No one climbs the ladder of success alone, and in my case I've always had a very strong sense of the presence of God and the support of my family.

Winning major tournaments in different countries – striving for recognition as a world champion golfer – is indeed the burning motivation of my professional life. This is what keeps me commuting from Johannesburg to Japan, the United States, Spain, Australia, England. And it is what makes it worthwhile to endure the pain of separation from my family and the loneliness of hotel rooms when I'm five, ten, or fifteen thousand miles away from home.

Yes, I have a strong desire to win – to be successful, but to me the true indicators of success in life are not money or even the individual achievements along the way. In fact, on my scale of priorities money takes the same place it does for Jack Nicklaus. After picking up a cheque for thirty thousand dollars for winning the Doral Eastern Open in 1972, he commented, 'Money's nice, it's essential, but winning major championships is my personal barometer.' And Lee Elder, the winner of the Monsanto Open in 1974, said, 'I don't worry about dollars. I just want to win another tournament and play better golf.'

Like Jack and Lee, I prefer to win. If I can't be first, I want to be second . . . I don't want to be 70th if I can be 69th. But even winning is not the final measure of success: I think that is really determined by the type of person you are . . . the quality of life you live. To put it in a very simple way, when I get to those big golden gates some day, I don't think someone up there is going to say, 'Gary, how much money did you make? How many putts did you hole? How many tournaments did you win?' Rather I think it will be, 'What sort of a person were you?'

# 9 Run for your life

*A physically fit person can do everything better.*

Physical fitness is **the** key to top performance and success . . . on the golf course, behind a desk, in the classroom, or in the kitchen. I know! It has been extraordinarily important in my own experience. There's no question in my mind that I escaped permanent injury when I broke my neck at age fifteen because my muscles and body were developed to such a fine point. However, exercise apart from skill will not produce a winner. But I'm absolutely confident of the fact that skill coupled with physical fitness – the ability to endure – is an unbeatable combination.

Unfortunately, though, this little paraphrase of the old Bible verse is so true, 'It's easier to get a camel through the eye of a needle than to get the average man to do any exercise.'

The average person's unwillingness to exercise for body health is something I've just never been able to understand. For example, most any businessman would be delighted to get a 10, 15, or 20 percent return on his investment. But I will guarantee a 1,000 percent return on an investment of only fifteen minutes a day spent in proper exercise. These are long odds. But it's true: a physically fit person can do everything better – thinking, working, playing, sleeping, reading – everything.

One of the best examples of physical fitness in the entire world of sports is veteran golfer Sam Snead. Today at age sixty-three Sam is competing effectively with men forty years younger. I just don't believe this can happen in any other sport, and this is why I believe Sam is the most incredible athlete in sports history. He has won over one hundred golf tournaments in his long and colourful career. And yet you can tee him up against anybody in the world today for eighteen holes, and he'll give a good account of himself.

How does he do it? Sam is the epitome of physical fitness. He may be sixty-three, but he has the body of a man of thirty-five. And he's out early in the morning exercising and jogging. A regular dynamo of energy and enthusiasm, Sam can stand in a doorway, kick his right leg up, and touch the board at the top with his foot. That's not an easy feat for even a very young man. But Sam is built like rubber and has a great sense of rhythm that comes from many years of participation in all kinds of sports.

Without a doubt Sam Snead is one of the nicest and most durable legends in the world of golf. In the course of his career he captured two PGA Championships, one British Open at St. Andrews, and three American Masters. But as yet the United States Open has eluded him. In 1937 he almost had it at Oakland Hills with a 283, only to see his chances slip away when Ralph Guldahl blasted previous records with a 281. Then in 1939 he took an eight on the 18th hole at Spring Mill, Philadelphia, when a five would have won the tournament. And in 1972 Sam finished only four strokes behind me when I took my second PGA Championship at Oakland Hills in Birmingham, Michigan – the same course where he had almost won the United States Open thirty-five years before.

Yes, Sam Snead is an amazing person – loaded with enthusiasm and a love for life, a superb example of a man who has invested wisely in physical fitness.

In my case I've already told how my father and brother impressed on me at an early age the importance of exercise and physical fitness as a means of achievement. To build up my legs I've skipped rope hour after hour, followed a steady routine of deep knee bends, and even today I try to run two or three miles four to five times a week. On occasion I still work out with weights and other exercising devices, and when I'm home I do a lot of physical work at my ranch. I never ask any man to do work I wouldn't do myself, so I've dug hundreds of post holes and put up fences and shovelled tons of manure.

To develop my arms and hands I do fingertip push-ups, chin myself on whatever is handy, swing weighted clubs or iron bars, and squeeze a small sponge rubber ball. But it all began when Ian made me pull myself up a rope anchored firmly to the high limb of the tree in our yard.

Frequently I'm asked to suggest a routine of exercise for today's business or professional man. And there's no doubt about it – one is needed. The sedentary life of most men in their thirties, forties, fifties, and sixties has made them unbelievably flabby and marshmallow soft. It is amazing how out of shape most people are. And because of it they are threatened with defeat in every area of life. The fact that such a high percentage of people go through life living at just a fraction of their physical potential is tragic.

My prescription is deceptively simple: When you get up in the morning, open a window, breathe deeply, and jog in place for fifteen minutes. At first you may be able to go for just five minutes, and then after a few days you can build up to ten. But the important thing is to stick with it until you can jog in place a full fifteen minutes every day, day in and day out. Of course, if you are situated so you can jog around the block or across country for fifteen minutes, so much the better. But if not, just run in place right inside your own home for fifteen minutes and it will change your life . . . you'll feel better physically, think more clearly, and be more stable emotionally.

The 'run for your life' slogan has become increasingly popular in recent years. Most every city has a 'run for your life' group or class at the YMCA. Running – jogging – increases the intake of oxygen throughout your entire body, stimulating blood circulation and building up the heart muscles. A book I recommend highly that can be found in most bookstores and that has been especially helpful to me is Dr. Kenneth Cooper's *Aerobics.* A vigorous advocate of jogging as a life-changing practice and founder of the Aerobics Centre in Dallas, Dr. Cooper tells in his book about a man who was given a medical discharge from the Air Force because of a bad heart and advanced arteriosclerosis – a thickening of the arterial walls which slows down the flow of blood through the body. Dr. Cooper put him on a jogging and exercise routine which in time completely cleared up the heart and artery condition, and the man was readmitted to the Air Force.

Walking briskly is a form of exercise available to most people. I know of men who drive their cars part way to work and then walk that last mile or so. This is an eycellent pattern to follow. But unfortunately, most of us will drive around the block a dozen times trying to find a parking place just a few steps from where we want to go. Ridiculous! And in my judgment that is just as silly as the golfer who rides in a cart while playing 18 holes. Run . . . walk . . . for your life.

An excellent exercise for the golfer is to swing a weighted club. Take an old driver and weight the head with lead. Swinging that weighted club regularly every day will strengthen the hand, wrist, arm, and back muscles. Another effective but simple hand and wrist exercise comes from squeezing a small rubber ball. I know of men who keep a ball in their desk drawer or in their car for this very purpose.

You will notice that none of the exercises I have recommended here are the least bit complicated or call for elaborate and expensive equipment. Not that barbells, stationary bicycles, and other exercise devices aren't good – it's just that the average person doesn't have them readily available. To meet the rigours of my own golf and travel schedule, I must be in top physical condition all of the time. Since I travel on planes, there is just no way to carry a lot of exercise equipment around. So the routine I've described here is a simple one. It works for me, and I wager that it will for you.

In addition to regular exercise, a proper diet is absolutely essential to physical fitness. Over the years the sportswriters have seemed to enjoy describing what they consider to be my eccentricities in food. And I suppose they have a point. One of my favourite breakfasts is sliced bananas, wheat germ, raisins, nuts, yogurt, orange juice, and raw oats all mixed together in a bowl. That combination may not appeal to anyone else, but these are all energy-producing foods, and it works fine for me. My basic diet, however, is made up primarily of meat, fish, vegetables, and fruit. I try to avoid fried foods, sugar, potatoes, white bread, rich desserts, coffee, and tea, and I never use milk except with my breakfast cereal.

Sensible and moderate eating habits and systematic exercise generate a vitality and zest for life that make you responsive and attractive to others. Everyone likes to be around people who bubble with enthusiasm and enjoy a good laugh. Though I've been accused of being too serious when I'm playing golf, off the course I'm as ready for a good time as anyone. But if you're out of shape and sluggish and feeling blah, you are far more likely to become irritable and moody. And there's just nothing more depressing and unpleasant than being around a grumpy and negative person.

Also I believe that both smoking and drinking are deterrents to good health and physical fitness. Frequently I'm criticized or put down for the directness of this statement. Don't think I'm being a goodie-goodie or a drum-beating moralist; I believe this strictly from the health point of view.

There seems to be considerable evidence today that smoking may cause cancer. But of even greater significance is its possible adverse effect on the heart.

The late nutritionist Adelle Davis points out in her books that alcohol in the system has a toxic effect and tends to break down body nutrients. She believes that the drinker evidences a marked loss of patience and an increased irritability when compared with the non-drinker. And I know professional golfers who have ruined their careers because of excessive drinking. It is true they might not admit that was the cause, but it certainly looks that way to me. At any rate, it seems silly to risk success in life by doing anything that might stand in the way.

Millions of man-hours a year are lost to industry and to the nations of the world because of needless illness incurred by the physically unfit. But even more important, millions of people in the world live way below their capabilities – are unhappy and depressed because they've neglected to build strong bodies that can endure the tensions and rigours of life today. To me, this is a senseless loss and a major evil. God has implied that our bodies are the temple of his Spirit. If this is true, and I think it is, it's important that our bodies be strong and virile and healthy – equal to the demands of any life-style. For me, that means being ready for whatever may be required of a professional golfer who each year crosses time zones and plays on courses throughout the world.

# 10 Partner in my life

*With faith in God a person's life can have more meaning.*

Faith is the most dynamic and energizing force in my life . . . faith in God, faith in other people, and faith in myself. For me, at least, the three are inseparable. And I'm grateful to my mother for helping me to understand at a very early age the importance of faith and belief in God.

In saying this I wouldn't want anyone to get the idea that I feel I've arrived at some lofty place or have achieved a special kind of goodness. That's just not true. And I'm probably more aware of that than anyone else. At least I know firsthand those places where I've failed to measure up or to reach the goals that are important to me.

In addition to my mother, three men have had a strong and lasting influence on my religious thinking. The first was Mr. Marcus Levy who came into my life for just a brief period of time when I was fifteen and had just started to play golf. Mr. Levy did two things that edged me toward a life-changing decision: he told me that with faith in God a person's life can be richer and have more meaning, that with faith incredible things can and will happen. Then he gave me a little book which I read eagerly. I'm not certain now of the title, but I think it was *Faith in Christ.* At any rate, it was then that I had a conversion experience and accepted Christ into my life.

Probably no person in the past twenty-five years has influenced more people around the world for God than Dr. Billy Graham. And I'm grateful to him for helping me come to a better understanding of prayer in a more practical way. One time when we were discussing this subject, I asked him, 'How does God hear and answer all the prayers that the millions of people around the world pray every day?' And he replied, 'Well, you know, it's just impossible for us with our tiny, finite minds to understand the greatness of God.' Then he made a very simple analogy that I found helpful: 'If you make a telephone call through the switchboard, there may be a great many other people talking on phones through that board at the same time and they're all getting through.' This reminded me of how quickly my long distance calls from America to South Africa are completed and how clear they are. It's just like talking to someone in the next room. How amazing it is that thousands and thousands of telephone calls go through very small wires simultaneously every day with proper connections being made at the other end of the line.

Naturally any attempt at explaining the dynamics of prayer is limited severely by our human understanding. But the important thing is that God does hear and care about what we feel and say. I'm very conscious of his presence in my life. And this is an absolutely tremendous thing when I think of the wonder and vastness of our marvellous and complex universe. It's almost unbelievable to think that the Creator of all this is concerned about me, Gary Player, and my needs. I recall reading somewhere an experience of one of the American astronauts who landed on the moon. Looking out into space toward earth, he was struck by the fact that it was so small a doubled fist extended in front of his eye could blot out earth completely. Imagine! And yet I believe that everyone of us on this tiny planet with all its problems is somehow important to God.

Several times over the past years Kermit Zarley, Babe and Jim Hiskey, and I have gotten Billy Graham to talk to the golf pros on tour. In one particularly appropriate talk he made an impressive and striking comparison between certain elements of golf and the Christian life. First he stressed the importance of a proper stance. The feet must be firmly grounded; body pointed in the right direction, properly poised and positioned to move in a rhythmic flow into the backswing and then down. As body, arms, and club uncoil, they can then release energy and power timed perfectly to the point of contact with the ball. And from the moment of impact the proper follow-through action takes over and the body turns to face directly toward the target. But essential to all of this action is the correct grip on the club itself. Just the slightest alteration of the grip will cause a bad shot even though all of the other action is correct.

Billy Graham then drew the analogy: the Christian must first adopt a correct stance, firmly committed to God's purposes and positioned through attitude and environment and direction to confront life. A proper club grip can be likened to a clear understanding of what one believes and his dedication to it. And any deviation can blur and mar the end result. The movement into the backswing is the commitment and abandonment to the process which finds its fulfilment in the action itself – living life creatively and relating to others redemptively – typified by the uncoiling of the body in the downswing and impact with the ball. And, of course, the follow-through is analogous to the truth that the Christian daily persists in those disciplines which help toward growth and maturity.

It was interesting to notice that even the pros who weren't believers enjoyed listening to him. One of them commented after the meeting that, though he wasn't a Christian, 'If anybody could convince me, it would be Billy Graham.'

In 1973 Billy Graham held a huge one-day Johannesburg crusade in our large sports stadium. It created a tremendous impact upon the city and thousands of people attended. As a matter of fact, this was one of the first (if not the first) great multi-racial meetings to be held in South Africa. On the afternoon before the crusade Vivienne and I held a large reception for Dr. Graham in our home. Our guests were entertained by a talented group of university students who sang several contemporary numbers. Then I introduced Billy and he talked informally to the group, primarily ministers – blacks, Indians, and whites. It was a truly integrated gathering; we had a wonderful time, and it was an ideal preview for the crusade.

*A recent family portrait, made when evangelist Billy Graham was a guest in the Player home. In front, left to right, are Wayne, Theresa, Michelle, and Mark. Behind them are Jennifer, Gary, Vivienne, holding Amanda Leigh; and Billy Graham. Gary acknowledges a tremendous debt of gratitude to Dr. Graham for helping him come to a better understanding of prayer in a practical way.*

Dr. Norman Vincent Peale, the minister of Marble Collegiate Church on Fifth Avenue in New York City, is the third person who has profoundly influenced my religious thinking. This happened first through my reading of his books. Then Vivienne and I met him personally when we attended his church. Following the service on Sunday morning Dr. Peale invited us into his study for a visit. This was a high moment since I had admired him from a distance for so long, but he surprised me by saying that he often watched me play golf on television and had been impressed with my positive attitude. He also said a very significant thing that I've never forgotten: 'If you surround yourself with people who are always miserable, you'll eventually become miserable and sour yourself. But, on the other hand, if you associate with people who are happy and positive and enjoy life, you will take on those same characteristics. Attitudes, like many diseases, are contagious.'

In so much of Dr. Peale's writing and preaching he talks about setting goals and visualizing positive results. It was reassuring for me to realize that this practice, which had already been so much a part of my life, really has its foundations in the Christian faith.

In November of 1973 when I was playing in the World Open Championship at Pinehurst Country Club in North Carolina, I read an absolutely amazing column written by Dr. Peale entitled 'The Importance of Being Astonished'. He told about visiting the British Museum in London and seeing a fragment of a papyrus scroll which had been discovered in the ruins of Oxyrhynchus, an ancient Egyptian city. According to experts the scroll is dated sometime before A.D. 300. And apparently it was part of a collection of sayings that were especially popular at the time.

In the column Dr. Peale says, 'But what is mainly interesting is not so much their origin, but the ideas which they convey. One saying begins: "Let him who seeks cease not from seeking until he finds, and when he finds, he shall be astonished. . . ."

'I think this states an extremely important truth – a truth which experience repeatedly bears out – that if you want something and go for it you will be astonished at the values you will find. . . . This bit of wisdom from many centuries ago tells us never to lose heart, never to stop seeking. It implies that if we have lots of patience and perseverance in seeking, not only will we find answers but much more wonderful answers than we had anticipated – so wonderful we will be astonished.'

Dr. Peale closed the column with this sage advice, 'Life holds in store, for every person who will look for them, discoveries so valuable that they are actually astonishing. Never accept anything less. Never cease seeking. Life will give you what you want if you keep after it.' (© 1973 by Creative Marketing Management, Inc.).

This is a truth which I believe deeply. Norman Vincent Peale and Billy Graham have helped me to understand it better, too, from the standpoint of the Bible through their emphasis on such verses as 'I can do all things through Christ who strengthens me' and 'the things which are impossible with men are possible with God.'

As a matter of fact, I've come to realize what an absolutely amazing and fascinating book the Bible is. It gives us, among other things, the pattern for living and for loving people. If I may say so, people around the world seem lonely and starved for attention and love and understanding. It is possible this may account for some of the hate, hostility, and suspicion that we see so much of today. Somehow if we could only learn to retaliate with love what a difference it would make!

I suppose the severest test to my own faith and attitudes took place in 1969 and 1970 when I was picketed and subjected to vicious abuse on the golf tour. Basically it was aimed against the apartheid policies of the government of South Africa. But the protest as it finally emerged was directed at me as a person without taking into consideration that I am not a racist and that I work constantly for understanding and improved relations between all races everywhere, and especially in my home country.

The bitterness and hate really surfaced at the 1969 PGA Championship which was played at the NCR Country Club in

Dayton, Ohio. Prior to the tournament a group of civil rights activists had threatened the city of Dayton and the Chamber of Commerce unless certain demands were met. Their idea was to embarrass the city at a time when a major sports event was being held. They picketed the tournament during the first two days without incident, but the harrassment emerged with a vengeance on Saturday during the third round.

Jack Nicklaus was my playing partner on this round. At the 4th tee as I was ready to hit my drive someone pitched a programme over the heads of the front-row spectators and it landed right at my feet. Then at the 9th green, just as I was poised for a par putt of eighteen inches, several people in the group shouted. My concentration had been broken and I missed the putt. Then, unbelievably, as I was walking toward the 10th tee, another demonstrator threw a cup of ice right in my face. I was stunned. Turning to him, I said, 'Well, what have I ever done to you, sir, that you would want to do that to me?' As he was escorted off the course by the police, he muttered, 'Damn racist!'

There was further disruption at the 10th green, with several people being arrested. In the midst of all this confusion Jack missed an eagle try, but I managed to sink a ten-foot putt for a birdie. The final bit of harassment that day came at the 13th green when a girl rolled a golf ball right up to my feet as I was getting ready to putt. In all, I think eleven people were arrested throughout the day.

On the fourth round I was paired with Raymond Floyd, who was leading me by just one stroke. Happily, we were free throughout the day from spectator interference. Ray and I see-sawed back and forth for the entire eighteen holes – first one and then the other of us would be in the lead. But when the last putt was holed, Raymond still was ahead by one stroke. Obviously I felt keen disappointment at losing, but believe me, I was really grateful to have done that well through all of the commotion.

Nevertheless, 1969 was a good year for me. I played in

sixteen United States tournaments, finishing fifth or better in ten and winning $124,000.

When it was time for me to return to the United States in the spring of 1970, the mood of some of the racial activists was still ugly, and threats of violence were actually being made. My advisors urged that I make a public statement to the effect that sports should be above politics. Among other things, I said, 'I will not criticize my country outside South Africa any more than an American would criticize America when away from home. Meanwhile I'm most grateful to be back in the United States to follow my profession – to play golf – and I do not feel I can offer any further political comment.'

At my first tournament, the Monsanto Open at Pensacola, Florida, four armed guards walked the course with me every day. Between March and May I played in eleven tournaments and those guards stayed with me all of the time. It was a frightening experience. I had no idea when there might be a crank in the gallery. I learned to accept worry as part of the routine of life.

Because of threats, reportedly from the Black Panthers, my Masters caddie, Ernest Nipper, felt he could not continue even though he had been with me for ten years. He was a fine person and a good friend. I hated to see Ernest go but understood his feelings. But in spite of the tension, this was my best United States tour up to that time – even though it was played under an oppressive cloud of fear and concern for what some irrational person might do or try.

Those were extremely difficult days, and it was hard to remain calm and relaxed. In fact, I don't think I could have in my own strength. But through faith and prayer, instead of meeting hate with hate, I tried to respond to the ugly mood in a spirit of love and understanding. I believe the demonstrators finally came to see that they were acting against the wrong person. God gave me such a feeling of security and love – it certainly wasn't something I could pump up myself – that I honestly didn't feel either malice or hate toward anyone. Happily, all of this is in the past now and is best forgotten.

While my golfing and travel schedule puts rigid restrictions on my time, I do enjoy speaking to young people and church groups whenever I can. I'm proud of today's youth; they seem to have a sincere concern for the future, and it is to be hoped that our world will become more secure because of them. It is unfortunate that press headlines concentrate on news of the rebels, who represent, after all, only a small percentage of the total.

Frequently I have the opportunity to meet with and speak to groups within the Fellowship of Christian Athletes. Hundreds of America's finest athletes are affiliated with the FCA. Close association with these people is a rewarding experience; I always enjoy being with them. It is reassuring to realize that most athletes, professional and amateur, are men and women of high moral integrity and many of them are committed Christians – this in spite of the antics of a few highly publicized swingers who like to boast about their risqué escapades.

One of the most awesome speaking engagements I ever had came in 1967 when I was invited to talk to the thirteen thousand ministers and messengers of the Southern Baptist Convention in Miami, Florida. And it was here that I received one of the greatest honours of my golf career: the Christian Athlete of the Year award. My message then was the same as it is now. I'm a professional golfer, not a theologian. But God is a partner in my life. And, as with any partnership, I'm sure he disapproves of some of the things I do and think. Still, the strength and guidance and motivation for everything I do comes from Him.

# 11 Golf is my business

*People ask what I do to keep busy . . .*

In my opinion, using golf clubs with fibreglass shafts in the 1965 United States Open was just about as great a feat as winning the title. Some time before that tournament, after some preliminary testing, I had signed a contract with the Shakespeare Company to use their fibreglass shafts. It wasn't long, however, before I began to have some second thoughts about their usability.

The association with the Shakespeare Company had been worked out by Mark McCormack upon the expiration of my initial equipment contract with First Flight. The First Flight relationship, which began in 1961, had been a most satisfactory and happy one. Nevertheless, when the Shakespeare Company, who were essentially manufacturers of fibreglass fishing rods, made the decision to expand their interests to include fibreglass shafts for golf clubs, they approached us with a substantial offer.

Before signing, however, Mark McCormack decided that in order to be completely fair to all parties, he should confer with both Jack Harkins, president of First Flight, and Henry Shakespeare. Held in Dallas, Texas, the meeting became the setting for what Mark describes as 'one of the funniest scenes I have ever witnessed in my business career.'

He brings the action hilariously to life in his book *The Wonderful World of Professional Golf:*

'Jack Harkins had brought along some First Flight clubs, and a handful of Shakespeare clubs. We had some clubs in the room, too. Jack was claiming that fibreglass was not strong enough material for a golf pro's golf club (an assessment that eventually proved to be correct), because there was excessive torque in the shaft. All of a sudden he stood up and said in his boisterous way, "These clubs have so much torque you can twist the heads right off them." Harkins was a very strong man, and he picked up one of the Shakespeare clubs, took the grip in his left hand and the head in his right and, sure enough, he twisted the head until it just about fell off the shaft. Well, that was more than Henry Shakespeare could bear. Henry jumped up and said, "You can take First Flight irons and you can bend them right over your knee like nothing," and he picked up one of Harkins' irons and bent it into an L just like he said. So Jack twisted off another head just to show how effortlessly he could do it, and Henry bent another iron, and pretty soon the argument was down to who could break the other guy's golf clubs using the least possible effort, and there were ruined golf clubs everywhere. As far as we were concerned Henry won the argument – with his money, not his clubs – and Player signed with Shakespeare.'

But as time passed it became increasingly clear that I just couldn't play consistently with fibreglass shafts, so after the 1965 United States Open our contract was terminated by mutual agreement.

Through my long association with Mark McCormack and his International Management Group, beginning in 1959, a plethora of business possibilities opened up. As people are becoming more aware in our Madison Avenue-oriented world, when a pro begins to win tournaments – and especially the major ones – opportunities emerge for business relationships which can be developed by an aggressive business manager. And, of course, I consider Mark the best. With the exception of South Africa, Mark is responsible for the exclusive conduct of my world-wide business affairs and career management and is ably assisted by Jay Lafave, Rick Isaacson, and others on his staff. But even in South Africa Mark plays a major part in assisting my longtime friend and associate Rex Evans in overseeing the affairs of Gary Player Enterprises. My relationship with Mark McCormack actually goes far deeper than business: our son Mark is named after him, and I am the godfather of his daughter Leslie.

One of my longest business associations in the United States is with the Puritan Sportswear Corporation of Altoona, Pennsylvania. The relationship with Puritan began in July of 1965 with my endorsement of their shirts, knitwear, and jackets. Slacks were added in 1971 upon the termination of a seven-year association with the Asher Slack people.

The distinctive black shirts and slacks I wear on the golf course are made by the Puritan people. There's been considerable speculation that I wear black out of superstition, and television announcers and newspaper reporters often refer to me as 'the Black Knight of the Fairways'. Actually, while some golfers wear the same shirt or glove or hat throughout a tournament for good luck, I think that's just a lot of nonsense; I don't believe in superstition. There's no real mystery: I wear black because it keeps me warm on cold and windy days, and I like it. It's probably true, too, that my taste for black clothes on the course has been influenced more than just a little by my love for western movies – those cowboys dressed in black may be the villains in the story, but they really look sharp.

I remember with a great deal of satisfaction one particular visit in 1971 to Puritan's plant in Altoona. In addition to a very pleasant time spent visiting with their thirteen hundred employees, I played an exhibition game of golf for them and shot a 62 on a par-72 course. That has to be a candidate for one of my best rounds of golf.

Since April of 1971 I have represented Dunlop golf clubs and golf balls for Dunlop Tyre and Rubber Corporation and am a member of the Dunlop International Golf Advisory Staff. Recently I've been involved with their technical people in the development and testing of a new Maxfli Red balata-covered golf ball which is nicknamed 'the Energy Ball'. In addition I'm associated with related Dunlop companies in South Africa, the United Kingdom, and Europe for golf ball representation only.

Other equipment relationships around the world include endorsements for golf clubs in the United Kingdom with John Letters and Company Ltd.; golf clubs, golf balls, and bags in Australia with Slazengers; clubs and golf balls for Campbell Manufacturing Company in Canada; wearing apparel for Teijin in Japan; and golf clubs in Japan with Daigin. Since I have won a total of fifteen tournaments in Australia numerous business possibilities have developed there. And in Japan I have nearly a dozen business relationships all of which consume quite a bit of my time and energy.

Some years ago Mark McCormack originated an innovative

*Gary with his manager, Mark McCormack, president and founder of International Management Group. The relationship goes far deeper than a business association; Gary's older son is named for McCormack and Gary is godfather to McCormack's daughter Leslie.*

programme which today is referred to as V.I.P. or customer golf. Presently we have contracts for customer golf with Chiquita Brands, Inc., of the United Fruit Company, the First National Bank of Chicago, the United States Banknote Company, and South African Marine Corporation. On a specified number of days each year I play rounds of golf with select customers of these companies. Not only is it usually a most enjoyable activity; I meet some very interesting people.

In addition to this book, my publishing activities include two editions of *395 Golf Lessons,* published by Digest Books in the United Kingdom and the United States. These have also been translated into Japanese and Afrikaans and are sold throughout the world. I've written two golf instructional books, and do the 'Gary Player Golf Class' – a strip appearing in the *Daily Express* in the United Kingdom and syndicated by King Features in the United States. And for some time now I've had an enjoyable association with *Golf* magazine as a member of their golf advisory staff.

A considerable portion of my time is given over to golf exhibition and pro-am matches and speaking engagements. Presently I average world-wide about thirty of these types of engagements a year involving a wide variety of groups. And in addition to occasional guest television appearances I've developed a set of four 20-minute golf instructional films which are available for purchase or sponsorship. Also in the autumn of 1974 a film entitled *To Be the Best,* my life story, was released for television in the United Kingdom. Hopefully, it will be seen on television in the United States.

In January of 1970 another dream burst into reality when I became an active partner in a golf course architecture firm now known as Kirby Player and Associates, Inc., with head-

(*Opposite page*) *Gary is an active partner in a golf course architecture firm, Kirby Player and Associates, Inc. Here Ron Kirby* (*on Gary's left*), *who was formerly an architect's representative for 7 years with the Robert Trent Jones organization, looks over a scale model and topographical layout with Pat Joiner* (*l.*), *Gary, and Dennis Griffiths* (*r.*).

quarters in Atlanta, Georgia. I first met my partner, Ron Kirby, in 1960 when he was associated with Paradise Island Country Club at Nassau. Then in 1963 he left Paradise Island and spent seven years as an architect's representative with the Robert Trent Jones organization.

Kirby Player's first project was to add nine holes to an existing eighteen at Atlanta's Berkeley Hills Country Club. Following that we put in an eighteen-hole course at Lake Lanier Island, north of Atlanta. But the exciting thing to me is that during the four years our firm has been in business we've established ourselves world-wide.

In 1970 we broke ground for our first course in Spain, and we have five more being constructed there today. And we presently have a course under construction at Mas Palomas in the Canary Islands.

We completed the first eighteen holes at Palmas del Mar for the Sea Pines Company in Puerto Rico in the spring of 1974. Chi Chi Rodriguez and I helped launch the grand opening in May. I consider it a great privilege to be associated with the Sea Pines Company as golf consultant and touring pro in the United States because of their enormous contribution to golf and to leisure activities in general. Those accomplishments can largely be credited to Charlie Fraser and Donald O'Quinn.

I'm also fortunate to be associated with La Manga Campo de Golf in Spain as director of golf. La Manga is located on the Mediterranean near Alicante on the east coast and is owned by my good friend Greg Peters.

Probably some of our most fascinating ventures are in Japan. Since the end of World War II, interest in golf has multiplied there many times over. In 1945 there were only seventeen courses in all of Japan; now there are over five hundred. Their triple-deck driving ranges are unique: golfers can actually hit practice balls from three levels. White balls come zipping off those three decks almost as if they were being shot from a hundred or so guns.

Our first golf course construction job in Japan was the eighteen-hole Odawara Golf Club at Odawara, and we now have five more courses under construction. At one of them, Nishi Nihon Country Club on the island of Kyushu, we are converting what was once an abandoned strip mine into a plush and beautifully landscaped eighteen-hole golf course.

Since only 16 percent of the land in Japan is arable, we're building courses on the most unlikely sites – on mountaintops or wherever we can find land that is unsuitable for anything else. An interesting illustration of our problem in building courses there is that we move an average of three million cubic metres of earth for an eighteen-hole course as compared to two hundred and fifty thousand cubic metres in the United States. And contributing to the complexities of the problem, there are two greens for every hole – one for summer play and one for winter. In other words, an eighteen-hole course has thirty-six greens. In contrast to the situation in the United States, it is not possible to alternate summer grass with winter grass on one green. Consequently, we plant bent grass on one green for winter and Korai grass on the other green for summer. This is the reason it usually takes longer to complete a course in Japan than anywhere else in the world.

I love the Japanese people and am very proud of my association with them. Japanese golfers are really improving; in fact, I consider them to be the best golfers in the world from fifty yards in, and they are tremendous putters. One of their outstanding professionals today is Jumbo Ozaki, who finished fifth in the 1973 American Masters. I enjoy playing the Japanese tour, which, in my judgment, ranks second only in size to the American. However, there is one disturbing thing to non-Japanese golfers: cameras are allowed right on the courses, and the click, click, click that goes on throughout a tournament is unbelievably distracting. One year Tony Jacklin played with earplugs all the time. But we find the building of golf courses in Japan to be a supreme test of our creative ingenuity, and I have many friends there whom I value highly.

In the United States we have either completed or are building courses in Florida, Tennessee, Georgia, New Mexico, and South Carolina. In designing a course our architects give careful consideration to the type of clientele who will be playing it, preferring to design courses that are interesting and fun to play. But I think probably one of the most unusual features of Kirby Player designs is that we are constantly looking for different ways to play the same hole. This means that we may design one or more alternate routes to the hole. For example, the 18th at Hilton Head Plantations, Hilton Head Island, is designed with two fairways. One fairway is a straight par 5 around a lake with little chance for anything under par. The alternate fairway offers a tight slot through trees to an exceptionally small landing area. In other words, if a player successfully executes his drive, he has a short second shot to the green with a definite eagle possibility or a sure birdie.

Frequently people ask what I do to keep busy on tour when I'm not actually practising or playing. The truth is – like most businessmen, I'm usually rushing frantically from one obligation or conference to another. Golf *is* my business . . . on the course and off.

# 12 Home: a very special place

*Zonnehoeve . . . Bellerive . . . South Africa*
*. . . the world . . .*

Home is very important to me. And even after four million miles of world travel, I'm never reconciled to being away. A telephone call home from my work usually averages about sixty dollars. As a rule, I'll call home at least once a week, and sometimes twice, although, if I've been away for an extended period, it's quite likely that I'll put through three or four calls a week.

Travelling the professional golf tour in the United States or Europe or Australia means lonely nights in all sorts of hotel rooms. And there's nothing that cheers me up so much as the sound of Vivienne's voice across the thousands of miles that separate us and hearing my children tell about the excitement of their day. While a telephone call is a poor substitute for being with them, it's the next best thing.

For me, home is our one-hundred-acre Zonnehoeve Plaas, located on a lush and beautiful site just twenty miles from Johannesburg, South Africa. Home is our fifteen-hundred-acre ranch, Bellerive, nestled in the picturesque Magoebaskloof mountains, two hundred and fifty miles north of Johannesburg. And home is South Africa, that delightful and controversial country perched on the southern tip of the African continent, bordered by the Atlantic Ocean to the west and the Indian Ocean on the east.

Zonnehoeve Plaas (Zonnehoeve is Dutch for 'place in the sun' and Plaas is 'farm') is one hundred acres of beautifully

manicured gardens, a swimming pool, an all-weather tennis court, thirty-five stables – ten for my own horses and twenty-five for rental – and a race track. Its population at the moment consists of one hundred horses – thoroughbreds and quarter horses – six dogs, a parrot, and one hundred and twenty pigeons. But most important, it is home for my wife, Vivienne, and our six children, Jennifer, Mark, Wayne, Michelle, Theresa, and Amanda Leigh. Believe me, no father was ever blessed with more wonderful children. Each is a unique and beautiful person.

Jennifer, our oldest, is fifteen – an effervescent girl with a great sense of humour and a special talent for music and horseback riding.

Mark is a strong and athletic thirteen-year-old. His interests are art, automobile racing, pigeons, animals, and sports. Like me, he is very serious about physical fitness.

Probably our most avid sportsman is Wayne, now twelve. I've seen few boys with a greater ball sense, and he plays good soccer. Wayne also has an amazing talent for golf; he shot a 47 for nine holes just the second time he played. He is also our sentimentalist, a trait he inherited from me.

Ten-year-old Michelle is our blue-eyed blonde – a good scholar and a superb gymnast and swimmer. When she was a little girl travelling with us in Scotland, Michelle saw a little furry animal with a bushy tail running across the lawn. Excitedly she asked 'What's that?' When I replied 'That's a squirrel' she immediately bubbled 'Oh I love squiddles.' From then on we've called her Squiddle.

(*Opposite page*) *Side view of the 14-room Player home at Zonnehoeve Plaas, 20 miles from Johannesburg. The one-foot-thick grass roof provides insulation so effective that summer air-conditioning is unnecessary and only minimum winter heating is required. Zonnehoeve, Dutch for "place in the sun" with Plaas, "farm", describes a site with 100 acres of gardens, a swimming pool, an all-weather tennis court and 35 stables.* (Photo by courtesy of Panorama.)

*Vivienne (holding baby Amanda Leigh) finds responsibilities heavy during the 6 months of the year that Gary is on tour. Fortunately, five older children are very protective of Amanda Leigh and help with her care: (l. to r. beyond Vivienne) Jennifer, Mark, Wayne, Michelle, Theresa.*

Every family has its little character, and in ours it is nine-year-old Theresa. I call her my little Indian because of her beautiful dark eyes. One of her greatest talents is smiling, but she's also an accomplished swimmer and horseback rider, and she loves to sing and play the guitar.

And finally, there's Amanda Leigh, the baby of the family, born on March 11, 1973. One of the great joys of my life was to be home when Amanda Leigh was born. I was with Vivienne through every moment of that great miracle of birth – and it is a miracle, one of the most profound in the human experience. The older children are very protective of Amanda Leigh and look after her with such loving and tender affection.

In spite of my travelling we are a close-knit and well-disciplined family. I believe it's important for a father to do things with his children – to *really* be with them – so we have a wonderful time playing baseball, tennis, and soccer. And we also do quite a bit of horseback riding and swimming. Playing together is a great builder of love and respect between parents and children.

It seems to me that the breakdown of home and family life is one of the greatest tragedies of our times. So often there is absolutely no communication between parents and children, and hostility is the only emotion that rises to the surface. Never is there any expression of love. And I'm convinced it is lack of love that produces so many drug addicts, delinquents, broken homes, and misery in the world today.

Despite the fact that my being away has been a hardship for Vivienne, I think we have an incredibly wonderful family life with, hopefully, just the right balance of discipline. I know she's had many lonely hours. Even though she travelled with me a great deal during the early years of our married life, every separation was painful. This was especially true in 1959 when our first baby, Jennifer, was born. I was playing in the American Masters at Augusta, Georgia, and just couldn't get home. Then in February 1961 I was in the United States on tour when Mark was born. Once again Vivienne was alone at a critical time – and I was alone when I wanted so much to be with her. But just three weeks after Mark's birth, Vivienne flew to Miami with him and Jennifer to be with me. It was a joyful reunion, and I saw my little son for the first time.

Within a few days after their arrival I won the Sunshine Open and two weeks later captured my first American Masters championship. In a way, my success in these tournaments helped alleviate the agony of our earlier separation. Never once, though, in the almost eighteen years of our married life has Vivienne complained about my going off. She's a marvellous mother and a wonderful, understanding wife.

Vivienne and I think it is tremendously important for our children to grow up with well-developed and disciplined minds and bodies, so we've made a rather unusual bargain with each of them. When they reach the age of twenty-one, if they have neither drunk alcoholic beverages nor smoked, we will give them a cheque for one thousand rand, about fourteen hundred dollars. And in addition, when they become twenty-five, if they still have refrained from smoking and drinking, we will buy each one a new automobile. I really believe this is one of the finest investments we can make in their lives.

The hub around which everything at Zonnehoeve moves is our fourteen-room brick home. One of its most unusual features, the one-foot-thick grass roof, may seem a bit strange to people in some parts of the world. But it is the best and most useful roof we could have, providing perfect insulation so that in the summer we don't need air-conditioning and in the winter very little heat is required for us to be comfortable. Our grass roof is maintenance-free and will hold up perfectly for many years. But its aesthetic quality is especially appealing – the exposed thatch on the inside is a rich golden colour, artfully accented by the black ceiling beams upon which it rests. On the outside the thatch is quite dark in colour, blending in beautifully with the surrounding landscape.

The second remarkable feature of our home is that every door opens out into a lush, green horse paddock. And for me it's a picturesque and restful sight to look out through any of our large French doors and see horses switching their tails as they graze contentedly on the grass.

I always feel a peculiar combination of peace and excitement during the two months or so we spend at home on our ranch in the breathtakingly beautiful Magoebaskloof mountains.

Named after a black chief, this area is one of the garden spots of South Africa. And I'm probably prejudiced, but I think the ranch itself is one of the most beautiful I've seen anywhere in the world. Situated six thousand feet above sea level, it is green all year, and the landscape is generously covered with tall, majestic pines, punctuated here and there by crystal clear lakes. Probably its scenic beauty is best compared to that in the state of Oregon in the northwestern part of the United States. We named the ranch Bellerive after a golf course that is very special to me – the course in St. Louis where I won the

*The stables at Zonnehoeve Plaas shelter 100 horses, among them some of Gary's racing thoroughbreds. Gary takes an active part in training and breeding stock.*

United States Open Championship in 1965 and thus became the third Grand Slam winner in the history of golf.

Bellerive, a working ranch, is ably managed by Dudley Mandy, a man who has become one of the closest friends I have ever had. Dudley's assistant, John Steel, is a newcomer, and Willie Betha, our black foreman, has worked faithfully on the ranch for thirty-eight years. Albert Rambouli, who helps run the stables, has a fine touch with the horses. These four men are responsible for the success of the ranch and each of them is a valued friend.

Enclosed with picturesque white fences reminiscent of Kentucky, Bellerive is the centre for our horse business. Here we have stables – all wired for stereo music – training rings, training and breeding centres, and a swimming pool for the horses. All of our feed is grown right on the ranch so we are completely self-sustaining.

I brought the first quarter horses into South Africa several years ago from the United States, and in addition we now have fifty thoroughbred horses which are trained for racing. These came from both the United States and Canada. After the thoroughbreds are trained at the ranch, they are moved down to Zonnehoeve where they are raced under the guidance of Bert Sage, his assistant, Arthur Sands, and five black jockeys.

Incidentally, one of the horses I'm particularly proud of is a four-year-old mare named Leslie Theresa. She is named Leslie after the daughter of my close friend and business manager, Mark McCormack, and Theresa after my own daughter. This horse came originally from Kentucky and during the past two years has won six of the seven races in which she has run. Leslie Theresa is one of my bright hopes for the future.

I really can't say that I have favourites among the horses, but I would like to give two others special mention. One is a handsome stallion named Maringoin, and the other is a chestnut we've named Plus Four because of his four white feet. Plus Four is by Maringoin and out of a mare whose grandfather was Tim Tam, a former winner of the Kentucky Derby.

*Gary never asks more of the men who work for him than he is willing to do himself. Loading grain with Gary are (l.) Willy Betha and (c.) Albert Rambouli, both valued friends as well as employees.*

(Photo by courtesy of Panorama.)

Bellerive is also a timber-producing ranch. The pines are grown and cut for lumber to be used in home construction and for making furniture. Actually the ranch is located in one of the fastest growing timber areas in the world because of the profusion of gentle warm days and a seasonal rainfall of approximately eighty inches.

Just recently we've added a herd of some six hundred sheep which we are raising for both meat and wool. Quite likely our most logical next step is cattle-raising, but it will be awhile before we start that. When we do, though, my choice will be Charolais.

Our entire family always spends the month of December at the ranch. This is a time I look forward to with great anticipation throughout the year. These wonderful days spent with our children are very special because they can never be recaptured. Together we ride horseback across the hills and valleys and under the tall pines. It is here my own spirits are rejuvenated and recharged for another year of world golf.

Several years ago when we learned from Jack Nicklaus that he planned to be in South Africa, we arranged for him to visit Bellerive. Both of us like to fish, and I'd been his guest several times on fishing trips in the United States. This was an opportune time to return the favour, so I had one of the lakes on the ranch stocked with trout. Unfortunately, we made the mistake of putting in too many, and the next thing we knew they began to eat each other because there wasn't enough natural food in the lake to support them. In desperation we had to fly special fish food in from Norway. When, after all this preparation, Jack and I were able to fish only a couple of hours, we had a good laugh over the whole thing. I guess if the expense were ever figured it would add up to a couple thousand dollars an hour. Just the same, it was worth it, because I've always enjoyed my friendship with Jack and was especially touched when he named one of his sons after me.

In late 1972 I expanded my ranching interests, and in partnership with my attorney, Bill Trollip, bought a fifteen-thousand-acre ranch down on the south coast of Africa in Cape Province at Plettenburg – about three hundred miles east of Capetown and seven hundred miles south of Johannesburg.

We bought the ranch originally just to grow pine trees for lumber and to raise cattle. But an interesting thing happened.

*King Protea blooms, this variety is pink with black edging. Protea bloom, South Africa's national flower, comes in a wide variety of colours in 126 species; the cut flowers last one month without water. Part of the expansion of Gary's business interest includes exportation of these blooms, grown on a recently acquired 15,000-acre ranch near Plettenburg in Capetown Province.*

Already growing on the land were thousands of the wild protea trees which produce the beautiful and colourful blooms that are the national flower of South Africa. We had been taking these trees out to plant pines, but one day on an impulse Bill

Trollip suggested that there might be a market for the blooms, so we consulted with an exporter in Johannesburg. He flew to Plettenburg and urged us to stop removing them and start planting the domestic variety so we could sell the flowers commercially. This we did, and by the end of 1974 we will have planted some sixty thousand domestic protea trees. Before long we hope to have three hundred thousand trees in production.

*Big Chet, prize quarter horse stallion, a gift to Gary from Dale and Chet Robertson.*

*Gary and Vivienne in the natural setting of Bellerive. Timber is one of ranch's chief products, as with the new ranch at Plettenburg.*

Protea blooms come in a wide variety of vivid colours in 126 species, and when cut, they last for one month without being kept in water. Now we export thousands of cut flowers to Germany where they are sold on the flower markets. Our future plans, of course, call for us to continue planting pine trees and raising cattle on the ranch, but in the meantime we are in the flower business on a grand scale.

Home is South Africa, a little known and frequently misunderstood country to so much of the world. Portuguese sailors were the first Europeans to sight South Africa when they rounded the Cape of Good Hope in 1488 in search of a water route to India. But the Dutch under Jan van Riebeeck were the first European settlers, arriving in 1652.

The Republic of South Africa is about three times the size of the state of California and the landscape varies dramatically. There are high plateaus, tall mountains, deep valleys, and picturesque beaches. Our great South African novelist Alan Paton movingly expresses the awe one feels at the beauty of the hills in Natal Province along the east coast: 'The grass is rich and matted, you cannot see the soil. . . . The ground is holy, being even as it came from the Creator.' And the climate is superb; our mean annual temperature is a pleasant and comfortable sixty degrees.

South Africa has one of the world's fastest-growing economies, with more gold and gem diamonds being mined here than in any other country of the world. And my home city of Johannesburg is right in the heart of the Witwatersrand, the richest gold field in the world. When you fly into Johannesburg, among the many striking sights you will see are the huge mountains of gold sand – the residue from the mines.

We have one of the most complex racial patterns of any

*(Opposite page) The Player family spend two months every year at their ranch home in the beautiful Magoebaskloof mountains, in one of the garden spots of South Africa. Left to right: Mark, Wayne, Michelle, Gary, Theresa, Vivienne, Jennifer.*

*Gary, at breakfast, lays out his plans for day.*

country in the world. Seventy percent of our population is black (Bantu), 18 percent is white, 3 percent is Asian, and 9 percent is a mixture of white, African, and Asian – usually referred to as Cape Coloured. Whites are outnumbered more than four to one by South Africans of colour. English and Afrikaans are the official white languages of South Africa, but many whites also speak at least one of the many black languages. While I'm not as proficient as I'd like to be, I can communicate quite well in the Zulu tongue.

It is in the area of race relations that South Africa has been severely criticized. Our situation is extremely complex and completely different from that in any other part of the world.

As in every other country, there are things that are obviously wrong, and a great many of us in South Africa are working hard to rectify them. I must say, however, that in all my travelling across the world I've never seen any country where white and black get along as well together as in my country.

But I firmly believe there are no problems in human relationships, irrespective of colour, that can't be solved when approached in a spirit of love and goodwill. Isolation does not achieve anything. I have high regard and affection for my many black friends in South Africa. And I was very proud several years ago when a group of black golfers organized the Gary Player Golf Club in Johannesburg. Actually there are more

*With Gary is Dudley Mandy, close friend and right-hand man, who is Bellerive's highly capable manager.*

blacks playing on the South African tour than in any other country in the world. We had fifty black players in the South African Open in 1974.

In 1973 Lee Elder, a black American golfer whom I greatly admire, came to South Africa and played in our PGA. I helped arrange for him to come and was proud of the reception he received. Lee and I played an exhibition match together, and he was given a standing ovation on the first tee. Everyone seemed to love him, and he was a great ambassador of goodwill for America.

Zonnehoeve is my home . . . Bellerive is my home . . . the vast and complex country of South Africa is my home. But in a very real sense the world has become my home as I have travelled across it so many times over the past eighteen to twenty years. For me, home is where my loved ones and friends are, and here there are no national or colour boundaries – the world is my home.

# 13 Turning point

*It was good to be back.*

A new year always means fresh beginnings and high hopes. We put past failures – and even past successes – behind us and reach out toward the future with optimism and anticipation, always confident the new year will be the best yet. At least this is the way I felt when 1973 rolled onto the scene.

But before the smell of newness had worn off even a little bit, my own private world tumbled into a dizzy spin. Consultation with my doctors in January had them insisting that I go into the hospital immediately for an operation. Anxiety and fear for the future filled every waking hour, and the fact that Vivienne was eight months pregnant only added to our distress. What would the operation mean for my future? And why should it happen now?

1972 had been a superb year on the tour for me. In addition to winning eight tournaments, I ranked number three on the World Money List with winnings of $219,599, and tied with Lee Trevino for third spot on the World Stroke Average Table with a 70.9 (Jack Nicklaus was first with 70.3; Peter Oosterhuis ranked second with 70.7). On the United States tour I had played in fifteen tournaments, averaging about twelve thousand dollars an event – all of this in my nineteenth year as a golf professional. This kind of record was my most effective rebuttal to the dire prediction of some golf prophets that at thirty-seven I might well be over the hill.

Now our hopes and goals for 1973 were threatened with

disaster. And on February 12th I entered the Suid Afrikaanse Hospital in Pretoria, thirty-six miles from Johannesburg, for major surgery. The ureter connecting my kidneys to the bladder was completely blocked, resulting in about 6 percent damage to one kidney. In a long and arduous operation four of the finest surgeons in South Africa, Dr. Hessa, Dr. Venter, Dr. Schulenberg, and Dr. Kloppers, corrected the ureter damage and also removed a cyst from the back of my left leg. Still, the big question that blocked out everything else in my mind was: what will this do to my professional golf career? I certainly didn't know, and at that point neither did anyone else.

My long days of convalescence provided ample time for reflective thought. Every physical need and wish was supplied by one of the finest and most professional staffs of nurses to be found in any hospital anywhere in the world. I just couldn't believe the dedication of those nurses and their aides. Though there is no way they can be adequately compensated with money, as a result of that experience, I want to salute nurses around the world, wherever they are serving.

During the days immediately following the operation I experienced considerable pain. This was a kind of adversity I had never felt before, but I thanked God for it. For nine days after surgery I had been unable to pass water because of the nature of the operation. Then on Sunday morning as the sound of beautiful organ music floated through the corridors and into my room, I was able to have relief for the first time. When I commented to one of the nurses about how good I felt and how much I appreciated the music, she explained that the organ was on loan to the hospital and would soon be returned. In my gratitude I made arrangements before leaving the hospital to donate an organ for the permanent enjoyment of the patients.

But while the nurses could care for my physical needs, no one else could possibly deal with my mental attitude. Lying there in that hospital room, I reviewed the past and pondered the future. This mental game began early every morning as the first brilliant rays of the sun began their dance across the sterile walls of my room. And it continued all day long until the declining reddish gold shafts gave way to shadowy announcements of approaching night, with its blinking lights and new sounds. Depression is a common experience for persons who have undergone major surgery, and most of us are ill-prepared for the long period required for complete recovery.

As my strength showed signs of returning, the nurses wheeled me out into the beautifully landscaped hospital gardens. Here the welcome scent of flowers and cut grass replaced the medicinal smells inside, and the cheerful counterpoint of bird songs took on new meaning, almost as if I had never heard them before. I was especially grateful for the seemingly little things that I'd come to accept as a matter of course in the day-to-day routine and pressures of life. Sights and sounds I'd missed for years suddenly flooded my senses, and I felt and responded to the love of Vivienne and each of our children with an exhilarating intensity. God was there; strength and vitality began to come back.

But the question still gnawed at my consciousness: what would all of this do to my future as a world golfer?

Except for the joy of being with Vivienne when Amanda Leigh was born, the days and weeks of convalescence dragged by with irritating slowness. My impatience and restlessness were almost at fever pitch when the time rolled around for the American Masters tournament in Augusta. I hadn't missed a Masters since 1957, and in sixteen tournaments I had won it once, placed second twice, and finished in the top ten a total of ten times. I like the Masters; it has always been good to me. Every tee box, fairway, and green was picture-clear in my mind. To miss it this year was spirit-wrenching agony, but I knew my body couldn't stand up to the rigours of tournament play.

My doctors finally cleared me to return to the United States tour in May, and I hurried to Atlanta. One thought crowded out everything else in my mind: Was I ready? . . . Could I make it?

During the weeks that followed I played in seven tournaments and made a miserable showing. In all, my entire winnings were only $12,000 – my individual tournament average the year before. Realizing that I was weak, I tried to hit the ball hard but couldn't get it past my shadow. Nothing worked, and my hook was the worst it had ever been. Jack Nicklaus, Lee Trevino, and others tried without success to prescribe a remedy.

It's hard to be away from home when you're playing well, but if you happen to be playing poorly, the sacrifice just isn't worth it. No amount of practice seemed to do a bit of good. By July I hit bottom – the low point of my entire career. Convinced there wasn't any use going on, I headed home almost sure that my professional golf career was over. Vivienne and I discussed the future, but she refused to give me advice one way or the other; the decision had to be mine.

For a little over a month I worked around Zonnehoeve and at the ranch, getting lots of exercise and rest. Strength soon began to flow reassuringly through the muscles and tissues of my body, and I really felt better than I had at any time since the operation. As I played my daily round of golf, the familiar rhythm returned. I realized my old touch was still there. Understandably, throughout this ordeal my father had been greatly disturbed. I recall saying to him one day while he was watching me practise, 'Don't worry, Dad. I'm healthy now and with the faith I've got I know I can make it. There's just no question.'

Determined to give it a try one more time, I flew back to the United States for the Sammy Davis-Greater Hartford Open at Hartford, Connecticut, where I played and hit well throughout the entire tournament. As a matter of fact, I was very much in contention until the 15th hole in the final round of play when a double bogey scuttled my chances and I dropped back, finishing the tournament in a tie for seventh place. Even at that it was good to be back in the top ten again.

But the Sammy Davis Open was highly significant for another reason. It was here that I worked out the change in my swing which cured a lifetime hook. Earlier a friend of mine in Johannesburg, Peter Matkovich, noticed that I was dropping my head as I went into my backswing and taking the club outside the line. He cautioned me to keep my head up and turn the club back on the plane. So, I concentrated on holding my head level and taking the club back with the natural turn of my body in the backswing. A deceptively simple step – but it worked.

A week later I won the Southern Open in Columbus, Georgia. From there I went on to place in the top ten in six more tournaments, and for the fifth time since its inception in 1964, I won the Piccadilly World Match Play Championship in October. Played in southern England on the 'Burma Road' West Course at Wentworth Country Club each year, this tournament has gained tremendously in prestige. Other winners include Arnold Palmer, Jack Nicklaus, and Bob Charles. In my opinion it now ranks fifth among the important tournaments in the world, and without question match play is the raw blood and guts of golf.

From the depths of depression in July to winning the Piccadilly World Match Play Championship in October of 1973 . . . this is the typically complex story of golf. Once again I enjoyed playing and was swinging better than ever before. And for the first time in twenty years I could push out of my mind any worry of hooking the ball.

# 14 In pursuit of the big ones

*'Pro golf . . . is a magnificent sport.'*

Eight years represents a rather sizeable slice of anyone's adult life. The years between my United States Open win at St. Louis in 1965 and the drama of 1973 were certainly no exception for me. The fact that I was still contending says something very important about those years as I've always insisted I would continue to play only as long as I was winning.

Although from 1966 through 1972 I won a total of thirty-four tournaments and placed in the top ten 67 times, the United States tour in the spring and early summer of 1968 was painfully frustrating. It is true that out of fourteen tournaments I placed in the top ten a total of ten times and had a United States stroke average of 69.9, but a winner's spot eluded me even though I came close two or three times. Of even greater concern was the fact that the Piccadilly World Match Play Championship in 1966 was the only major championship I'd been able to take since the 1965 United States Open.

It was with this less than impressive showing that I went to Carnoustie in July 1968 for the British Open. In spite of everything, including the fact that Carnoustie is one of the world's most difficult courses, I felt exceptionally optimistic. Did I say 'one of the world's most difficult courses?' Actually, I have since rated it *the* hardest course I have ever played anywhere.

Located on the Angus coast of eastern Scotland just a few miles from Dundee, Carnoustie is a small resort town with full

*Gary studies his drive to the 18th green during the third round of the 1974 American Masters at Augusta National Golf Club. At this point Gary was tied for second place with 8 under par.* (Wide World Photos.)

exposure to the turbulent and capricious North Sea. It enjoys a long and rich history in the world of golf. However, its modern era actually began in 1872 when Tom Morris enlarged the original course from ten to eighteen holes. The course now stretches to a full 7,252 yards of unbelievably narrow and rolling fairways, strategically placed bunkers with sand the consistency of fine dust, and treacherous deep roughs. Although every hole on the course is of killer quality, the final three are downright diabolical. Both the 17th and 18th fairways are crisscrossed three times each by a winding stream called Barry Burn. Carnoustie is truly a course to test the mettle of a champion.

Since putting had seemed to be a major weakness during the United States tour, I phoned Vivienne and asked her to bring my old blade putter with her when she flew up from Johannesburg to join me. This putter had served me well from the time I bought it in Japan for fifty dollars in 1961. In the United States I could probably have purchased it for five dollars in any pro shop. But in 1966 I had started using a Ping. Possibly switching back to my old friend would sharpen my putting game and bolster my confidence on the greens.

On the first round of tournament play I had a 1.30 p.m. starting time, and while the day had started off clear and without wind, by mid afternoon the weather had deteriorated badly. It was a battle all the way, and I closed out the round with a 74. There was just one consolation – most of the other scores were high: Jack Nicklaus finished with a 76, and Arnold Palmer limped in with a discouraging 77.

Happily, the weather eased off on the second day and the scores dropped at a startling rate. Billy Casper turned in a searing 68 and Jack Nicklaus thundered back into contention with a 69, while Palmer and I each turned in a 71. In general I was putting much better than in previous tournaments.

An eagle on 14 and a birdie on 18 offset some other problems to give me a 71 for the third round. Casper, who had been leading the tournament by four strokes, faltered and finished with a 74. My second and third rounds of 71 each now had me

*Golf is often a game of strong emotions, as shown in these photos of Gary.*

in strong contention just two strokes behind Casper.

Weather on the final round turned cold and the wind was sharp – as sharp as the action. Casper bogied number 2, narrowing his lead to one stroke. Then while I was taking a birdie on 6, Casper bogied 5, moving me up with a one-stroke lead for the first time in the tournament.

By the time I reached 14, Billy Casper and Bob Charles had evened things up and we were tied at two over par. My drive on 14 cut right down the middle of the fairway in perfect position. Selecting a 3-wood, I laced into the ball; the shot was so straight I had to lean sideways to see the top of the flag stick. The green was elevated just enough that I couldn't see the ball, but Henry Cotton excitedly held up his two hands indicating it had stopped just two feet short of the hole. Vivienne had been sitting in the stands at 14 waiting for me to come up. Ian Reid of the *Daily Express,* with whom I do the golf strip lessons all over the world, told me later that just before the ball completed its descent to the green she began a piercing scream that didn't let up until the ball rolled to a stop. If there is such a thing as a 'career' shot, I guess this one qualifies. My tap-in for an eagle gave me a two-stroke lead. I'll never forget that hole as long as I live . . . it is nicknamed the 'spectacles hole' because two well-placed bunkers right in front give it the appearance of a pair of eye glasses.

Pars on the next four holes brought me in with a 73 and a total score of 289 – just two strokes ahead of Jack Nicklaus, my playing partner, and Bob Charles. For the second time I had captured the prized British Open Championship – just nine years after my first win. I was deeply moved when we got back to the Bruce Hotel and the entire staff joined together in singing 'For he's a jolly good fellow'.

Following the British Open I went on in 1968 to win six more tournaments, including the World Series of Golf at the Firestone Country Club in Akron, Ohio, and the Piccadilly World Match Play Championship. My third victory in the World Match Play at Wentworth was especially satisfying in that it retired the trophy – a replica of the statue of Eros in London's Piccadilly

*Jack Nicklaus grasps Gary around the shoulders following Gary's win in the 1968 British Open. Bob Charles, at Nicklaus's right, tied for second with Jack at 291, two strokes behind Gary's 289. The tournament was a close battle all the way, with Billy Casper (who led at beginning of final round) also in strong contention.*
*(Photo by Alan Clifton for SPORTS ILLUSTRATED © Time Inc.)*

Circus. It is rather interesting that when the tournament was originated, the officials ruled that any player who won three times could keep the trophy permanently. Doubtless they thought no one would. But with this win I took the trophy back to Johannesburg with me, and they had to go out and buy another one.

The year had given me tournament victories in England, South Africa, the United States, and Australia – a further step toward the fulfilment of my lifelong goal of being rated as top world-class golfer. In addition, I placed eighth on the World Money List with winnings of $130,012.56 and ranked third in World Stroke Average with 70.19 behind Jack Nicklaus (70.11) and Billy Casper (70.15). And winning the British Open for the second time gave me the first leg of the second Grand Slam. With this one behind me I could now concentrate on the remaining three.

It began to look as if the fates had joined forces to deprive me of that second leg in the next Grand Slam. During the years of 1969, 1970, and 1971 I won a total of thirteen tournaments, but the three big ones remained just beyond reach. My hopes were high for the United States PGA in 1969, but I was forced to settle for second place. In 1970 I placed third in the Masters, and in 1971 was tied for fourth in the PGA. On the World Stroke Average Table, I placed second in 1969 with 70.494 and third in 1971 with 70.3. The statistics were favourable; I was playing well, but it just wasn't enough. Another three years had slipped by, and while every one of the thirteen tournament wins was important to me, my fourth Piccadilly Match Play Championship remained the major achievement.

But 1972 reversed that trend and gave me that long desired second leg of the four big ones. It was the month of August and the setting was Oakland Hills Country Club in Birmingham, Michigan, a fashionable suburb of Detroit, the host for the 56th United States PGA Championship. In peak physical condition, I was eager to take on Jack Nicklaus, the defending champion, and a superb field of some of the world's finest golfers.

The 7,054-yard course at Oakland Hills couldn't have been in finer condition, and its 118 bunkers were to cause excruciating difficulty to more than one player, myself included, during the four days. Without doubt Oakland Hills is one of the five greatest courses in the world, and the greens superintendent does a tremendous job maintaining the course. A battle was in the making that would thrill the 110,000 fans who lined the fairways and greens.

As is so often the case, the leader after the first round of tournament play on a wet and soggy course was a young and comparative newcomer – Buddy Allin, who carded a fine 68. Crowding Buddy at 69 were Arnold Palmer, Jim Jamieson, Jerry Heard, Larry Gilbert, and Ray Floyd. I closed out the day with a 71, one stroke ahead of Nicklaus and two strokes up on Lee Trevino and Billy Casper.

The usual musical chairs shift of positions occurred on the second round. Although it was a beautifully clear day with a brilliant blue sky, that didn't seem to help Palmer and Nicklaus a bit as they dropped back with disappointing 75s. Jerry Heard took the lead at the halfway mark, and I hovered three strokes back at 142, having shot my second 71.

Five birdie putts on Saturday ranging from eight to thirty feet gave me a round of 67, one stroke into the lead with a three-round total of 209. But Casper, Heard, and Brewer were breathing heavily down my neck. That one-stroke lead was too narrow for comfort.

Finding my optimism dampened by a light but steady rain on Sunday morning, I decided to give my spirits a boost with a telephone call home. After I had talked with Vivienne and the children, my father came on the line and said, 'Win it for me, Gary.' Thinking back over his years of sacrifice and support, I made up my mind to do just that if it was humanly possible.

But I got off to a start almost as dismal as the day with three bogies and a birdie on the first four holes. The lead seesawed back and forth among several contenders for the first fourteen or fifteen holes.

For me, the 16th was the decisive hole and determined the

*Gary assesses the requirements for a fairway shot.*

outcome of the tournament. My approach shot had to be made from 150 yards out, and a tall tree blocked my view of the flag stick which was positioned at the extreme side of the green just beyond a water hazard. There was no way I could see the flag, but, fortunately, a spectator had left a seat stick right in line with the hole. Selecting a 9-iron, I sighted my shot with the seat stick and hit the ball out of the wet grass. It cleared perfectly and rolled to a stop just three feet from the hole, leaving a makeable birdie putt. This gave me a two-stroke lead over Jamieson and Aaron. It hadn't been easy, as I'd gotten into just about every kind of trouble that can plague a golfer in tournament play.

A 7-foot putt for par on 17 gave me some anxious moments, but it dropped into the cup as if attracted by a magnet. An easy par on 18 wound up the tournament for me with a two-stroke lead over the nearest contenders and a total of 281. Jim Jamieson and Tommy Aaron were tied for second at 283 while Sam Snead and Ray Floyd shared a 284.

That second PGA victory had been won for Dad. The nineteen years from 1953 to 1972 had been arduous and marked with many unforeseen turns and detours. Along the way I'd become associated with some of the finest athletes and golfers in the world. I'm proud of my profession and I agree wholeheartedly with an observation Mark McCormack makes in his book *The Wonderful World of Professional Golf:* 'Pro golf . . . is a magnificent sport, unsullied by scandal, free of the deadly excesses of chauvinism, uncrippled by growing pains. Its financial rewards are great, but its players have not demeaned themselves in the pursuit of them. Through good management and good luck, pro golf has kept the one characteristic that is central to its history: class. It offers us, and always has, the highest sort of sporting drama – man against himself.'

# 15 A year of high drama

*As long as I can win . . .*

On the final day of the 1974 Masters at Augusta National Golf Course, my caddie, Eddie McCoy, and I were standing in the middle of the 17th fairway waiting to hit my approach shot to the par-4 hole – the 71st of the tournament. Eyeing the green, I commented, 'Eddie, in seventeen years at the Masters I haven't hit this green but six times, yet this is where I won the tournament in 1961. We're going to win our second one on this hole today.'

Selecting a 9-iron, I hit the ball directly on line with the flag stick, and while it was still in flight, I said, 'Eddie, we aren't going to have to putt this one.' But we did – the ball rolled to a stop no more than six inches from the cup. My tap-in gave me a birdie three and a two-stroke lead with just one more hole to go.

I went to the Masters in April 1974 strong in the belief that I could win it. Even though I hadn't competed in many tournaments during the early part of the year, I had already won two: the Dunlop Masters, for the fifth time, and the General Motors Classic – both on the South African tour.

By the end of the first round of play the leaderboard showed Jim Colbert one stroke in the lead with a 67. Hale Irwin, Hubert Green, and Don Iverson were right on Colbert's heels at 68. And in a five-way tie for third spot at 69 were Jack Nicklaus, Don Sikes, Frank Beard, Ray Floyd and Gene Littler. I posted a one-under-par 71.

*Gary shakes the hand of his caddie Eddie McCoy, after winning the 1974 American Masters with 4-day 10-under-par total*

(Wide World Photos.)

Dave Stockton dominated the second round. His searing 66 nosed out even Hale Irwin, who set a Masters record by shooting five birdies in a row from the 12th through the 16th holes. For the second straight day I finished with a 71, but I was terribly frustrated because I'd played well even though my putting was off – 72 putts for the two rounds.

Moving into the third round on Saturday, I experienced a great surge of confidence because I felt certain my putting would improve. At the end of the first eleven holes I stood at one under par and was playing exceptionally well. Then followed a string of five birdie putts: one foot on 12, fifteen feet on 13, seven feet on 14, twenty feet on 15, and six feet on 16. This tied Hale Irwin's record of the first day for the same five holes and moved me to within one stroke of the lead.

After parring 17 I moved on to 18, where my approach shot to the green insured a birdie possibility that could put me into a tie with the leader, Dave Stockton. But as I was lining up my putt, a frightful thing happened: one of the spectators right on the edge of the green collapsed with an apparent heart attack. Naturally there was a great deal of confusion as several people shouted for an ambulance. At the moment, of course, there was no way of knowing how serious the man's condition was, but I learned later that he died.

Stepping back from the ball, I was really shaken. It was scary; I didn't know whether to putt or wait. Fighting to regain my concentration, I moved back over the ball and lined up the putt again, but it missed by inches. A par on 18 gave me a three-round score of 208, one stroke behind Stockton.

Sunday dawned hot and humid. This had been a good week so far at Augusta and the course had never played better. As I moved up to the first tee, the feeling that I could win the tournament was very strong. I'd been playing some of the best

*(Opposite page) Gary with his family prior to opening day of the American Masters tournament. They all flew from Johannesburg to Augusta except baby Amanda Leigh, then thirteen months old. Standing behind their parents are (l. to r.) Michelle, Jennifer, Theresa, Wayne, and Mark.*

*Gary strikes a tee shot during the 1973 Piccadilly Match Play Tournament.* (Syndication International.)

(*Opposite page*) *Gary sizes up a putt.* (Syndication International.)

golf of my career and was working hard, and when I work for something, I expect it to happen.

A birdie two on the 6th hole brought me up even with Dave Stockton. Then I took the lead on the 9th after hitting a 6-iron to an extremely difficult pin placement . . . the ball rolled to within ten feet of the cup, and I holed it with a birdie putt.

Jack Nicklaus had started the day five shots behind Stockton and four behind me, but he launched a threatening charge throughout the early holes. A fifty-foot eagle putt on 13 moved him up to within one stroke of my lead. But he faltered with bogies on 14 and 16.

Then came the drama on 17 which gave me a two-stroke edge and my second Masters championship. My four-round score of 278 was the fifth best in the history of the tournament, and I'm still the only non-American golfer to win the Masters. And if I'm not mistaken, I am the only golfer in the history of the Masters tournament who has scored 280 or better on five occasions. With this win I had taken my seventh major tournament, and the $35,000 purse pushed me over the million dollar mark in United States winnings – an accomplishment reached by only five others at that time.

Actually, though, I would have passed the million dollar mark long before except for the fact that, according to regulations, winnings from the World Series of Golf, a tournament I've won three times, are not computed in official career earnings. But, to me, this is not important. The money list doesn't even begin to tell the true story. Because of smaller purses in the past, such top golfers as Hogan, Snead, and Nelson don't rank very high in total earnings. In my opinion there are golfers on today's circuit that have won a great deal more money than Hogan who aren't even equipped to carry his clubs.

The thrill of winning, of achieving a goal is tremendously important. But this time I was especially happy because

(*Opposite page*) *Gary on the fairway during the 1973 Piccadilly Match Play.* (Syndication International.)

Vivienne and five of our six children were in Augusta to share with me in the excitement of the victory. They are my greatest fans, and their support is a strong element in my determination to win.

Also I want to make special mention of my regular Masters caddie, Eddie McCoy. He is a superb caddie and gave me the same kind of helpful encouragement which Rabbit provides in other tournaments. Because of his help and positive attitude I gave Eddie a cheque for $3,500 so he could buy a new truck which was needed badly in his regular work as a carpenter, a set of Gary Player golf clubs, and some clothing.

Winning the Masters naturally raised speculation about my chances of taking all four of the Grand Slam tournaments in one year, a feat that has never been accomplished. Ben Hogan made a run for it in 1953 and took three of the four. But that year he didn't even compete in the PGA. And in 1972 Jack Nicklaus captured the first two, the Masters and the United States Open, but lost his chances when he dropped the British Open by one stroke. Jack insists that it is next to impossible to make a one-year Grand Slam, but to have that first leg was a great encouragement, and I was determined to try.

I go into each major championship with that particular tournament as the only immediate goal. My schedule for the whole season is built around the major tournaments, and I'd rather win one of them than twenty of the regular ones. So, it was only to be expected that my thoughts skipped over the next several tournaments to focus on that first week in June when the United States Open Championship would be played at Winged Foot Golf Club in Mamaroneck, New York. If I could win it, that would give me a double round on all the major championships and the second leg in my try for the Grand Slam in a single year.

*(Opposite page) Gary with the Piccadilly Match Play Trophy, the fifth time he has won it.* (Syndication International.)

Upon leaving Augusta I flew immediately to La Manga, Spain, for the Spanish Open. And from there I went on to Japan to play in a tournament before flying home to Johannesburg for a rest and time with my family.

In May I returned to the United States for the Colonial Invitational at Fort Worth, Texas, and a five-week swing that would climax with the United States Open in Mamaroneck.

But a happy thing occurred on the way to the Open – the Danny Thomas-Memphis Golf Classic, played on the Colonial Country Club course in Memphis, Tennessee. On the first day of this tournament Rod Curl and I led the field with rounds of 65 each. Hubert Green took the lead on the second day and clung to it tenaciously until the 12th hole of the final round when I holed a bunker shot for a birdie. Added to the birdies I'd just made on 10 and 11, that incredible shot on 12 gave me a one-stroke advantage. From there I went on to win the tournament and its $35,000 purse with a four-round total of 273, fifteen under par and two strokes ahead of Hubert Green and Lou Graham, who tied for the second spot at 275.

Winged Foot Golf Club at Mamaroneck is one of the toughest and most brutal courses on which a United States Open is played. Since 1959 was the last time I had played the course, I went up a week early to play a round or two before going to Philadelphia for the Classic. Built in old-fashioned style, Winged Foot has tight fairways and small, well-trapped greens. A golfer can't just stand on a tee there and bang away but must think and know how to place his shots. Never has there been a tougher test given to United States Open golfers than by this course. In fact, so great is my respect for it that one of the best horses I've ever bred in South Africa is named Winged Foot.

The first day of the United States Open was oppressively hot. And it became obvious right at the start that the par-70 course would be hard to beat, so I was grateful to lead the field by one stroke with a 70 on the first round. But after the first day I began to slip. Winged Foot took a heavy toll at the 36-hole cut by eliminating such names as Lee Trevino, Billy Casper, Gene Littler, Tony Jacklin, and Tommy Aaron.

A field of the world's finest golfers fought gamely to conquer the course in this year of 1974, but Winged Foot fought back with stubborn vigour to produce 72 holes of heartache, agony, and bruising frustration. At one point Jack Nicklaus commented, 'These are the most severely undulating greens I have ever seen. They have obviously driven everybody up a tree.' And for the most part the course refused to give up sub-par rounds. Very few were recorded during the four days, and when the final putt was holed, it was Hale Irwin's championship with a seven-over-par 287. My 293 placed me in a tie for eighth spot and doomed my chances at that point for either a second career Grand Slam or a possible 'big four' in one year.

Disappointed? Yes, of course. But long ago I learned there is just one thing to do after losing a tournament – forget it. That is what the game of life is all about: facing the adversity of defeat and then going on to the next task. The important thing was that I was playing excellent golf – and only twelve months after the lowest point in my career.

Wednesday, July 10, 1974, marked the first day of the 103rd British Open Championship, played this year on old Royal Lytham and St. Annes, a course which skirts the Irish Sea at Blackpool on the Lancashire coast. It also marked my twentieth consecutive start at the Open.

Since the British Open is the only one of the four major tournaments that admits the regular touring caddies, I had decided some months earlier to take Rabbit Dyer with me. He had never been out of the United States so I knew it would be a great experience for him. This was one way I could express my great appreciation for Rabbit's loyalty to me. Back in 1973 when everything looked bad and I was at my lowest, he gave me nothing but encouragement. At one point I even suggested that he caddie for someone else and make more money. He wouldn't hear of it, and I'll never forget his encouraging words: 'No, laddie, you're my man. There's a whole barrel of money

out there in the future, and we'll get it.'

Rabbit was the first black caddie to appear in the British Open. And it created a sensation from the moment he landed. When a startled customs official checked one of his suitcases and found it full of a special type of American horseshoes, Rabbit had to explain they weren't for good luck but for my thoroughbred horses. From then on, Rabbit became quite a celebrity in his colourful pants and straw plantation hat. He has a great sense of humour, and I thought one of his remarks to a reporter was a classic: 'I suppose I'm different. I guess I look like a fly in a glass of buttermilk.'

Royal Lytham is another one of those British Open sites that is lashed by cold and fickle crosswinds. Every one of its 6,822 yards is tough; the knee-deep roughs are unbelievably hazardous, and 224 bunkers guard just about everything in sight. Actually the walls of those bunkers are layered with sod that has been tiered up like bricks. One of the golfers said that bricklayers must have built the walls of the traps. Since the first British Open was played at Lytham in 1926 and won by Bobby Jones, the course has hosted four more Championships. One of those, I am proud to say, was won by my fellow South African, Bobby Locke.

Mischievous winds and rain tormented the first round of play on Wednesday. And for the first time a British Open was being played with the more wind-resistant large American ball (which measures 1.68 inches as compared to 1.62 inches for the British ball).

In my opinion, I came close to playing a perfect first round, even with a double bogey on 17. Thanks to four birdies on the front nine, I closed out the day with a two-under-par 69 and in a tie for first with John Morgan, a British club professional from Stoneham.

*(Opposite page) Gary and Rabbit display the Player clubs before the start of the 1974 British Open.* (Syndication International.)

*The Player grip, as displayed during the 1974 British Open.*
(Syndication International.)

(*Opposite page*) *Gary playing superbly from a bunker.*
(Syndication International.)

A grinding wind plagued Thursday's round. Wind is a distinctive part of the British Open, making it a different kind of golf from anywhere else in the world. But I enjoy playing under those conditions. Upon completion of the first nine holes, I was two under par. And after picking up one more stroke on the back nine, I closed out the round with a 68, making a two-round score of 137 – five strokes ahead of Peter Oosterhuis and my South African friend Bobby Cole at 142. Incidentally, I have read a great deal about how good some of the young American golfers are, but in my opinion Bobby has the best looking swing of them all.

In addition to the wind, Lytham was exacting its vengeful toll in other ways. My partner for the first two rounds was Hale Irwin, the reigning United States Open champion. He was absolutely stunned at the different course conditions; one of the other golfers said it must be like playing on the moon.

Twenty thousand spectators lined the course and filled the stands for the third round of play. Expectations ran high; there were eighteen holes of golf to play – and play them I did, but not with the finesse of the first two days. From the 9th hole on I experienced trouble that added up to a four-over-par 75. Nevertheless, I still held the lead by three strokes with a 212. Peter Oosterhuis was at 215, and Jack Nicklaus had surged into third place with 216.

For three days I held the lead – a frightening and nerve-wracking experience. Now the stage was set for that final round. And because tee-off frequently runs as late as 3 p.m. in the British Open, a golfer has much more time to work up a good case of nerves. It is amazing what vivid pictures one's mind can dream up between early morning and the beginning of a round of play in mid-afternoon.

My concentration was so intense that at times it seemed as if I were in a trance. In fact, this was true throughout the entire

(*Opposite page*) *In conference with Alfred Dyer* (*Rabbit*) *during the 1974 British Open.* (Syndication International.)

PLAY

tournament. For example, one time while on the practice tee, I was so deep in concentration that when Jack Nicklaus walked up I asked him how he'd done and was amazed when he replied that he hadn't even been out on the course yet.

The weather on Saturday seemed a good omen, with the temperature hovering in the upper 60s. A gentle breeze replaced the fierce wind of the other days, and fleecy white clouds dotted an otherwise brilliant blue sky.

Peter Oosterhuis was paired with me, and I got off to a good start with a birdie on the par-3 first hole. This happens to be another one of Lytham's peculiarities – a par-3 first hole. But it was a good one for me as I had birdied it three times in four rounds of play. Going on from there I birdied the second hole and took a par on 3. Bogeys at 4 and 5 shaved the edge somewhat. But a long-iron second shot put me within seven feet of the flag stick on the 6th hole, and a well-stroked putt gave me an eagle three. A birdie on 7 and pars on 8 and 9 produced a front-nine score of 32, three under par and five strokes ahead of Oosterhuis.

On the return nine – that part of the course which gave everyone fits all week – I took pars on 10, 11, and 12 . . . birdied 13 with a chip-in . . . parred 14. A bogey at 15 dropped me to four under par, and I held that through 16.

But as so often happens, the drama of the tournament occurred on the last two holes. A fine tee shot on 17 put me in excellent position, but my 6-iron second shot went wild and landed in knee-deep rough. Unable to spot the ball, we began a frantic search. I called out to everyone around, 'Please come help me find the ball.' I had to get down on my knees like a little whipped pup as I pawed the grass looking for the ball. Just sixty seconds short of the five-minute limit, one of the marshals located the ball. My 'thank you very much' was the understatement of the year. Had we not found it in the specified time, I would have incurred a costly two-stroke penalty.

The grass was so high and tough that even though I was only twenty feet from the hole I took a full swing and moved the ball just six feet. A very deep cut in the ball attested to the

*Gary in the rough on the 18th hole of the 1974 British Open.*
(Syndication International.)

strength of the swing and the sharpness of impact. When I walked off the green with a miraculous 5, I should have looked up that marshal, thanked him again, and given him two dozen golf balls as a token of my appreciation, but I guess my mind was just on that last hole. Later when I mentioned to Bob Rosburg that I'd like to find the marshal, he said, 'Forget it. If you advertise for that man now, you'll have fifty takers.'

On the 386-yard par-4 18th hole, after teeing off with a 1-iron, my 5-iron second shot pounded through the green and came to rest right up against the old brick wall of the clubhouse. From my spot down the fairway I couldn't see the lie, but it was obvious even from there that the ball was well beyond the green.

Words can't even begin to express how I felt as we walked up to the 18th green. Fifteen thousand people packed the stands which ringed two sides and the back of the green, and they stood up and clapped for a solid ten minutes. All week long the galleries were courteous and enthusiastic; a record crowd of 90,625 had supported the tournament. But that spine-tingling applause at 18 prompted one particular picture to fill the screen of my mind. For a split second I saw a Roman gladiator standing proudly over a fallen lion in the centre of an arena accepting the thunderous plaudits of thousands. It was a tremendous moment and one for which I will be grateful for the rest of my life.

After examining the position of my ball, I felt certain the officials would rule in favour of a drop. But they insisted that since it was not a hazard or ground under repair, the ball must be played from where it was. Fortunately, the ball was slightly plugged in the dirt and as I hit it left-handed with my putter, it popped out over the flowerbed wall and rolled to a stop on the green just ten feet from the cup. Two putts gave me a bogey five for the hole . . . a two-under-par 282 for the tournament . . . and the winner's spot by four strokes over Peter Oosterhuis at 286. Jack Nicklaus held sole possession of third at 287 with Hubert Green one stroke behind at 288.

*A tense moment at the 1974 British Open. At Lytham St. Annes, England, as Gary makes a left-handed shot with his putter from the wall at the back of 18th green. Though he finished this hole with a bogey, Gary won the tournament with a 72-hole total of 282, two under par.* (UPI Telephoto.)

*The Trophy is held aloft as a proud Gary wins the British Open for the third time.*
(Syndication International.)

(*Opposite page*) *Gary kisses the trophy following the 1974 British Open, his third victory. This victory, with his previous wins in 1958 and 1969, gives him one British Open per decade.*
(UPI Telephoto.)

Minutes later, as I stood at the edge of the green before television cameras, I became acutely aware of the significance of that moment. Flags of twenty-seven nations fluttered proudly in the breeze. Golfers from many different countries had participated in this important event; golf with its international flavour had brought all these people together. And in the emotion of the moment I said something which I believe deeply: 'It bothers me that some countries are not open to people of every race and creed. But I have great feelings of warmth and gratitude for Great Britain and America because they welcome everybody.'

Immediately following the presentation ceremonies, my daughter Jennifer, Rabbit, and I hurried off to our rented house for dinner before catching the train for London. While we were eating, a photographer from one of the newspapers stopped by to take a picture of us with the trophy. Believe it or not, in our excitement we had failed to bring the trophy with us – it was still back at the clubhouse. Rabbit and the photographer dashed back and retrieved it while I packed. Moments after the photographer got his picture, we hurried off with the trophy and caught the train just before it started to move out of the station.

Winning the 1974 British Open Championship gave me victories in three different decades – 1958, 1969, and 1974; the only other person to achieve that was Harry Vardon. It was also my 8th major title, and the 99th overall, in pursuit of my goal of becoming the best golfer in the world.

Recognition for one's effort is always a rewarding experience,

*In the history of golf, only four men have won all four tournaments of the sport's Grand Slam—the British Open, the United States Open, the United States PGA, and the American Masters—and none has done so in a single year. Pictured in a display at Golf's Hall of Fame in Pinehurst, North Carolina, are* (*top left*) *Ben Hogan,* (*top right*) *Gene Sarazen,* (*lower left*) *Gary Player, and* (*lower right*) *Jack Nicklaus.*
(Photo courtesy of Golf Hall of Fame.)

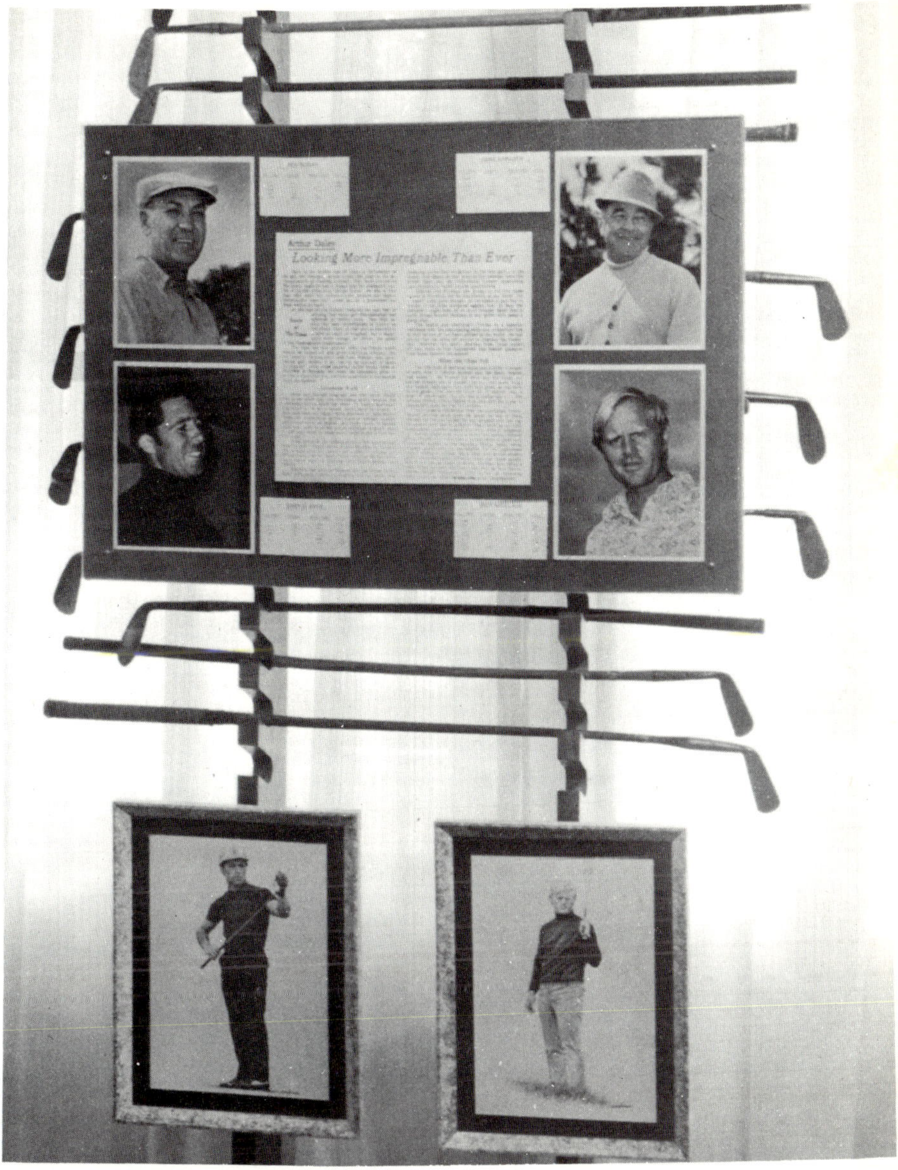
Arthur Daley
Looking More Impregnable Than Ever

and I'm deeply grateful for the honours that have come to me in the twenty-one years of my professional golf career. But on September 11, 1974, in ceremonies held at Pinehurst, North Carolina, induction into the World Golf Hall of Fame moved me deeply. It was a high honour to be included on this first list of such outstanding golfers as Walter Hagen, Ben Hogan, Bobby Jones, Mildred 'Babe' Zaharias, Byron Nelson, Sam Snead, Gene Sarazen, Harry Vardon, Patty Berg, Arnold Palmer, Jack Nicklaus, and Francis Ouimet. In a pre-ceremony announcement of this significant event, President Donald C. Collett of the World Golf Hall of Fame said, 'We think this will be one of the most memorable days in the long, long history of golf. To have assembled at one time these greats of the game is a sight that perhaps has never happened before nor ever will again.' For this South African it certainly was!

How long will I compete? I don't know . . . but only as long as I'm playing well enough to win. I believe I've done well so far because of hard work and my faith. In reality, faith has been the primary guideline of my life. But when I'm playing a tournament, I don't pray to win. Probably most of the players are doing that. After all, there can be only one winner, and there's no special reason God should pick me to win. Rather, I pray for courage, strength, and guidance, and the ability to go on loving *everyone.*

## A PERSONAL NOTE

One of the serendipities of my years as a book publisher, editor, and writer has been the association with interesting and creative people. The infusion of their ideas and personalities into my life has brought enrichment and fulfilment to my own style.

Working with Gary Player on this book has indeed been an experience which I treasure. His sanguine attitude is contagious . . . his love for life is an inspiration for greater effort . . . his thoughtfulness for others builds confidence . . . and his faith in people and in God is an inspiration. Above all, he is a 'thorough gentleman' – the highest accolade he himself can give to another man. It is not an exaggeration to say that having gotten to know him and share in his experiences has made me a richer person. For this I am deeply grateful.

*Floyd Thatcher*
*November 1974*

## CAREER STATISTICS

| *Year* | *Tournaments Won* | *Finished in Top Ten** |
|---|---|---|
| 1955 | East Rand Open (South Africa) | |
| | Egyptian Match Play | |
| 1956 | East Rand Open (S.A.) | |
| | Dunlop Tournament (England) | |
| | South African Open | |
| | Ampol Tournament (Australia) | |
| 1957 | Australian PGA | |
| | Coughs Harbour Tournament (Australia) | |
| 1958 | Natal Open (S.A.) | |
| | Australian Open | |
| | Kentucky Derby Open (U.S.) | |
| | Ampol Tournament (Australia) | |
| | Coughs Harbour Tournament (Australia) | |
| 1959 | Transvaal Open (S.A.) | Memphis Open, 2nd (tie) |
| | South African PGA | |
| | Victorian Open (Australia) | |
| | British Open | |
| | Natal Open (S.A.) | |
| | Western Province Open (S.A.) | |
| | Dunlop Masters (S.A.) | |

*Statistics unavailable before 1960

| Year | Tournaments Won | Finished in Top Ten |
|---|---|---|
| 1960 | South Africa Open<br>South African PGA<br>Dunlop Masters (S.A.)<br>Transvaal Open (S.A.)<br>Natal Open (S.A.)<br>Western Province Open (S.A.) | American Masters, 6th (tie)<br>Greensboro Open (U.S.), 5th<br>Houston Classic (U.S.), 4th (tie)<br>Sam Snead Festival (U.S.), 6th<br>Eastern Open (U.S.), 2nd |
| 1961 | American Masters<br>Lucky International Open (U.S.)<br>Sunshine Open (U.S.)<br>Yomiuri (Japan)<br>Ampol Tournament (Australia) | Milwaukee Open (U.S.), 4th (tie)<br>Colonial National Invitational (U.S.), 7th (tie)<br>San Diego Open (U.S.), 3rd<br>Tucson Open (U.S.), 4th<br>Baton Rouge Open (U.S.), 3rd (tie)<br>New Orleans Open (U.S.), 3rd (tie)<br>Pensacola Open (U.S.), 2nd<br>St. Petersburg Open (U.S.), 3rd<br>U. S. Open, 5th (tie)<br>'500' Festival Open (U.S.), 3rd<br>Portland Open (U.S.), 4th (tie)<br>American Golf Classic, 2nd<br>Seattle Open (U.S.), 3rd<br>Los Angeles Open (U.S.), 4th (tie)<br>Houston Class (U.S.), 8th (tie)<br>Tournament of Champions (U.S.), 6th (tie) |

| | | |
|---|---|---|
| 1962 | United States PGA Championship<br>Australian Open<br>Transvaal Open (S.A.)<br>Natal Open (S.A.) | American Masters, 2nd<br>Memphis Open (U.S.), 2nd (tie)<br>United States Open, 4th (tie)<br>St. Paul Open (U.S.), 3rd (tie)<br>Western Open (U.S.), 3rd (tie)<br>San Diego Open (U.S.), 5th (tie)<br>'500' Festival Open (U.S.), 5th (tie)<br>Seattle Open (U.S.), 5th |
| 1963 | San Diego Open<br>Australian Open<br>Transvaal Open (S.A.)<br>Sponsored 5,000 | Los Angeles Open (U.S.), 2nd (tie)<br>Crosby National Pro-Am (U.S.), 2nd (tie)<br>Palm Springs Classic (U.S.), 2nd<br>Phoenix Open (U.S.), 2nd<br>Pensacola Open (U.S.), 2nd (tie)<br>American Masters, 4th (tie)<br>Colonial National Invitational (U.S.), 2nd<br>British Open, 7th (tie)<br>Memphis Open (U.S.), 3rd<br>United States Open, 8th (tie)<br>United States PGA Championship, 6th (tie)<br>Utah Open (U.S.), 3rd<br>New Orleans Open (U.S.), 4th<br>Greensboro Open (U.S.), 5th (tie)<br>Thunderbird Open (U.S.), 5th (tie)<br>Cleveland Open (U.S.), 5th (tie)<br>American Golf Classic, 8th (tie)<br>Whitemarsh Open, 6th (tie) |

| *Year* | *Tournaments Won* | *Finished in Top Ten* |
|---|---|---|
| 1964 | Pensacola Open (U.S.) | Tournament of Champions (U.S.), 5th (tie) |
| | '500' Festival Open (U.S.) | Phoenix Open (U.S.), 3rd |
| | South African Masters | American Masters, 4th |
| | | Whitemarsh Open, 2nd |
| | | Carling World Tournament, 3rd |
| | | Colonial National Invitational (U.S.), 4th (tie) |
| | | Cleveland Open (U.S.), 6th (tie) |
| | | Canadian Open, 5th (tie) |
| 1965 | United States Open | American Masters, 2nd |
| | South African Open | Pensacola Open (U.S.), 5th (tie) |
| | World Cup Team | Buick Open (U.S.), 8th (tie) |
| | Australian Open | Thunderbird Classic (U.S.), 2nd |
| | Piccadilly Match Play (England) | World Open, 4th (tie) |
| | NTL Challenge Cup | Philadelphia Open (U.S.), 4th (tie) |
| | World Series of Golf | |
| | World Cup International Trophy | |
| 1966 | Piccadilly Match Play (England) | Jacksonville Open (U.S.), 3rd |
| | South African Open | Colonial National Invitational (U.S.), 6th (tie) |
| | Natal Open (S.A.) | Oklahoma City Open (U.S.), 6th (tie) |
| | Transvaal Open (S.A.) | British Open, 4th (tie) |
| | | United States PGA Championship, 3rd (tie) |
| | | Thunderbird Invitational (U.S.), 6th (tie) |
| | | Canada Cup, 6th (tie) |
| | | Dunlop International (Australian), 8th (tie) |
| | | General Motors Open (S.A.), 3rd (tie) |

| | | |
|---|---|---|
| | | South African PGA Championship, 3rd (tie) |
| 1967 | Dunlop Masters (S.A.) | Greater Jacksonville Open (U.S.), 9th (tie) |
| | South African Open | American Masters, 6th (tie) |
| | | Oklahoma City Open (U.S.), 2nd |
| | | Memphis Open (U.S.), 6th (tie) |
| | | Greater Hartford Open (U.S.), 3rd (tie) |
| | | Westchester Classic (U.S.), 4th |
| | | Carling World Open, 3rd |
| | | Thunderbird Invitational (U.S.), 10th (tie) |
| | | British Open, 3rd (tie) |
| | | Australian Open, 8th (tie) |
| | | Dunlop International (Australia), 8th (tie) |
| 1968 | British Open | Pensacola Open (U.S.), 4th |
| | World Series of Golf | Greater Jacksonville Open (U.S.), 7th (tie) |
| | Piccadilly World Match Play (England) | Greater Greensboro Open (U.S.), 9th (tie) |
| | South African Open | American Masters, 7th (tie) |
| | Natal Open (S.A.) | Azalea Open (U.S.), 2nd |
| | Western Province Open (S.A.) | Byron Nelson Classic (U.S.), 4th (tie) |
| | Australian Wills Master | Greater New Orleans Open (U.S.), 9th (tie) |
| | | Colonial National Invitational (U.S.), 4th (tie) |
| | | Atlanta Golf Classic (U.S.), 7th (tie) |
| | | Canadian Open, 10th (tie) |
| | | Cleveland Open (U.S.), 9th (tie) |
| | | Thunderbird Classic (U.S.), 5th (tie) |
| | | Australian Open, 2nd |

| *Year* | *Tournaments Won* | *Finished in Top Ten* |
|---|---|---|
| 1969 | Tournament of Champions (U.S.) | Monsanto Open (U.S.), 5th (tie) |
| | South African Open | Greater Jacksonville Open (U.S.), 3rd (tie) |
| | South African PGA | Greater Greensboro Open (U.S.), 5th |
| | Australian Open | Colonial National Invitational (U.S.), 2nd |
| | Australian Wills Master | Atlanta Classic (U.S.), 3rd |
| | | Western Open (U.S.), 5th (tie) |
| | | Kemper Open (U.S.), 3rd (tie) |
| | | Greater Milwaukee Open (U.S.), 2nd |
| | | United States PGA Championship, 2nd |
| | | General Motors Open (S.A.), 4th |
| | | Dunlop International (Australia), 3rd |
| 1970 | Greater Greensboro Open | Monsanto Open (U.S.), 8th (tie) |
| | Australian Open | American Masters, 3rd |
| | Dunlop International (Australia) | Greater New Orleans Open (U.S.), 6th (tie) |
| | | Tournament of Champions (U.S.), 2nd (tie) |
| | | Houston Champions International (U.S.), 4th |
| | | Atlanta Classic (U.S.), 3rd (tie) |
| | | American Golf Classic, 8th (tie) |
| | | Sean Connery Tournament (England), 9th (tie) |
| | | Lancome Tournament of Champions (France), 4th (tie) |
| | | Dunlop Masters (S.A.), 2nd |
| | | General Motors Open (S.A.), 2nd |
| | | South African Open, 7th |

**1971**

Jacksonville Open (U.S.)
National Airlines Open (U.S.)
General Motors Open (S.A.)
Western Province Open (S.A.)
Dunlop Masters (S.A.)
Piccadilly World Match Play (England)

United States PGA Championship, 4th (tie)
American Masters, 6th (tie)
Tournament of Champions (U.S.), 2nd (tie)
Colonial National Invitational (U.S.), 7th (tie)
Atlanta Classic (U.S.), 3rd (tie)
Kemper Open (U.S.), 2nd (tie)
British Open, 7th (tie)
Wills Open (Scotland), 4th (tie)
Dunlop Masters (Wales), 5th (tie)
Lancome Trophy (France), 2nd
South African Open, 2nd
South African PGA (Fall), 4th (tie)
Australian Open, 7th
Dunlop International (Australia), 9th

**1972**

United States PGA Championship
World Series of Golf
Greater New Orleans Open (U.S.)
Dunlop Masters (S.A.) (twice)
South African Open
NCR Western Province Open (S.A.)
Japan Air Lines Open
Brazilian Open

Florida Citrus Open (U.S.), 10th (tie)
American Masters, 10th (tie)
Atlanta Classic (U.S.), 2nd
Kemper Open (U.S.), 4th (tie)
Canadian Open, 10th (tie)
British Open, 6th
Lancome Trophy (France), 3rd
Lan Manga International Pro-Am (Spain), 6th (tie)
South Africa International Classic, 2nd
Louis Luyt PGA Championship (S.A.), 3rd
Jackie Gleason Inverrary Classic (U.S.), 9th (tie)

| *Year* | *Tournaments Won* | *Finished in Top Ten* |
|---|---|---|
| 1973 | Southern Open Championship (U.S.) | Sammy Davis, Jr.-Hartford Open (U.S.), 7th (tie) |
| | Piccadilly World Match Play (England) | Heritage Golf Classic (U.S.), 5th |
| | Dunlop Masters (S.A.) | John Player Classic, 4th (tie) |
| | General Motors Classic (S.A.) | Lancome Trophy (France), 3rd (tie) |
| | | South African International Classic, 4th (tie) |
| | | South African PGA, 6th (tie) |
| | | Chunichi Crowns Tournament (Japan), 5th (tie) |
| 1974 | American Masters | World Series of Golf (U.S.), 2nd – Lost to Lee Trevino in play-off |
| | British Open Championship | Piccadilly World Match Play Championship (U.K), 2nd |
| | Australian Open Championship | South African PGA Championship, 2nd |
| | Brazilian Open Championship | Wills Masters (Australia), 2nd (tie) |
| | Memphis Classic | Dunlop Masters (U.K.), 2nd – Lost to Bernard Gallacher in play-off |
| | Dunlop Masters (S.A.) – Won over Bobby Cole in play-off | Spanish Open, 2nd |
| | La Manga International Pro-Am (Spain) – Won over Clive Clark in play-off | South African Open, 4th |
| | Ibergolf Trophy (Spain) – Won over Peter Townsend in play-off | Colonial National Invitational (U.S.), 6th |
| | General Motors International Classic (S.A.) | United States PGA Championship, 7th |
| | Rand International Open (S.A.) | United States Open, 8th (tie) |
| 1975 | South African Open | Dunlop Masters (S.A.), 4th |
| | | Tournament of Champions (U.S.), 2nd – Lost to Al Greiberger in play-off |

## ACKNOWLEDGEMENTS

I am especially grateful to my wife, Vivienne, for the help and support she has given me over the years and for her encouragement in doing this book. And special thanks are due my sister, Wilma Jacobs, for her invaluable assistance in bringing together many of the photographs which are so important to the story.

We are indebted to Mark McCormack and his associates for their assistance. The *World of Professional Golf Annuals* for the years 1968 to 1972 and *The Wonderful World of Professional Golf*, all by Mark H. McCormack, were particularly useful in checking times and events.

Others whose help has contributed to the success of this book include Norma M. Smith, librarian, World Golf Hall of Fame; Philip R. Wahl, manager of Augusta National Golf Club; Dean Matthews, manager of Bellerive Country Club.